PENGUIN BOOKS
THE BEST OF LAXMAN
THE COMMON MAN CASTS HIS VOTE

Rasipuram Krishnaswamy Laxman was born in Mysore in 1924. He began cartooning for the *Free Press Journal*, a newspaper in Bombay, in 1947, soon after he graduated from the University of Mysore. Six months later he joined the *Times of India* as staff cartoonist; he continues to draw for the newspaper even today.

R.K. Laxman has written and published numerous short stories, essays and travel articles, some of which have been collected in the book, *The Distorted Mirror*. He has also written three works of fiction, *The Hotel Riviera*, *The Messenger* and *Servants of India*, all of which have been published by Penguin Books. Penguin has also published several collections of Laxman's cartoons in the series The Best of Laxman and Laugh with Laxman. *The Tunnel of Time*, Laxman's autobiography, is also available from Penguin.

R.K. Laxman has won numerous awards for his cartoons, including Asia's top journalism award, the Ramon Magsaysay Award, in 1984. The University of Marathwada and the University of Delhi have conferred honorary Doctor of Literature degrees on him. In 2005, the Government of India honoured him with the Padma Vibhushan.

R.K. Laxman lives i

R.K. Laxman

THE BEST OF LAXMAN

The Common Man Casts His Vote

PENGUIN BOOKS

PENGUIN BOOKS
Published by the Penguin Group
Penguin Books India Pvt Ltd, 11 Community Centre, Panchsheel Park, New Delhi 110 017, India
Penguin Group (USA) Inc., 375 Hudson Street, New York, New York 10014, USA
Penguin Group (Canada), 90 Eglinton Avenue East, Suite 700, Toronto M4P 2Y3
Penguin Books Ltd, 80 Strand, London WC2R 0RL, England
Penguin Ireland, 25 St Stephen's Green, Dublin 2, Ireland (a division of Penguin Books Ltd)
Penguin Group (Australia), 250 Camberwell Road, Camberwell, Victoria 3124, Australia (a division of Pearson Australia Group Pty Ltd)
Penguin Group (NZ), cnr Airborne and Rosedale Roads, Albany, Auckland 1310, New Zealand (a division of Pearson New Zealand Ltd)
Penguin Group (South Africa) (Pty) Ltd, 24 Sturdee Avenue, Rosebank, Johannesburg 2196, South Africa

Penguin Books Ltd, Registered Offices: 80 Strand, London WC2R 0RL, England

First published by Penguin Books India 2005

Copyright © R.K. Laxman 2005

All rights reserved

10 9 8 7 6 5 4 3 2 1

Typeset by S.R. Enterprises, New Delhi
Printed at Chaman Offset Printers, New Delhi

INTRODUCTION

Just over a century ago the art of cartooning came to India from England and struck roots. Although other forms of art like sculpture, poetry and painting had flourished in our country for centuries, the art of graphic satire and humour was unknown. Of course both satire and humour did exist in folklore and popular poetry, poking fun at the follies of men and monarchs; the funny antics and humorous articles of the court jester were really satirical comments used to gently bring a wayward king and his band of courtiers back on track.

The role of today's cartoonist is not unlike that of the court jester of yore. His business in a democracy is to exercise his right to criticize, ridicule, find fault with and demolish the establishment and political leaders, through cartoons and caricatures.

When the British ruled, the freedom allowed to the press was limited. The role of editorial comments and cartoons was largely confined to tackling social evils like child marriage, child labour and the dowry system, or praising the efforts of the reformers. They hardly ever touched on political subjects.

Some years later the Indian cartoonist began to make timid forays into political matters. But he confined himself to attacking symbols—John Bull, for instance. When our struggle for independence from imperial domination began to gather momentum, the cartoonist gained the courage to depict real characters: the political leaders, and the viceroys and governors who were the guardians of imperial authority. Enslaved India was symbolized by an image of a suffering Indian woman called Bharat Mata—a semi-divine being adorning a crown with flowing black tresses wearing a carefully draped sari. The lady did indeed serve the purpose of inspiring patriotism in the heart of the people, inviting them to free themselves from the shackles of British imperialism.

When the British left, our leaders, who had fought for independence, settled down to draw up a respectable Constitution which would ensure freedom and equality for people who had been denied democratic liberty for centuries. India was declared a sovereign secular republic in which every citizen would enjoy liberty, equality and fraternity. The freedom of the press became particularly sacred. It was one of the most important checks to be imposed on our democratic institutions. Having drawn up such a magnificent Constitution, the leaders and the led sat themselves down and looked forward to a life of peace and prosperity.

If things had worked the way our founding fathers had hoped, the cartoonist would have become an extinct species long ago. But fortunately for the cartoonist, both the rulers and the ruled unintentionally became champions of the cartoonist's cause and ceaselessly provided grist to his mill.

When Nehru took over as Prime Minister, it soon became apparent to the cartoonist that he could look forward to an exciting career ahead. The aspirations of linguistic chauvinists, cow-protectors, prohibitionists, name-changers of parks and streets, all began to make their ludicrous appearance on the national scene. Our political activities became equally uproarious from the satirist's point of view. Our leaders introduced an altogether new style of functioning in our political life—hitherto unknown to the ordinary citizen. News about political parties did not concern their ideologies or their plans to help the common man, but detailed instead how intra-party groups worked against each other, squabbled amongst themselves, parted company from the party to form a new one, or defected to the very party they had opposed tooth and nail until that very moment. All this led to curiouser and curiouser political behaviour—dharnas, floor-crossing, booth-capturing, 'toppling' a chief minister, and what have you. Naturally, a cartoonist, even one with limited talent, could flourish effortlessly in this atmosphere. So, within a decade of independence, the tribe of cartoonists proliferated. New dailies, weeklies and fortnightlies published in every feasible language mushroomed everywhere, thus opening up vast opportunities for the cartoonist.

As a nation we are rather prone to talk politics—whether at a bus-stand or in a railway compartment, hobnobbing at an exclusive cocktail party or jogging in a public park. Of course, what passes for politics in these sessions is really gossip—rumour, hearsay or scandal rooted in some blurred misrepresentation of facts—concocted into a palatable mixture that is masticated between reading newspapers and magazines and listening to political news on the radio or television. That is why, though not all Indian publications are political in content, most allow for a page or two of political satire and caricature, in acknowledgement of our national pastime. Thus, the country that didn't have a single cartoonist less than a century ago is now swarming with them: good, bad and indifferent.

As I became more and more entrenched in watching and commenting on the political phantasmagoria of our country I needed an acceptable symbol to define the common Indian in my cartoons. For the cartoonist, time is of the essence and the political cartoonist has the Damocles' sword of deadlines hanging permanently over his head. Many precious minutes would be lost if I were to draw elaborate masses of people composed of Maharashtrians, Bengalis, Tamilians, Punjabis and Assamese. It is easy for the cartoonist in the West where the dress and appearance of people are largely standardized, but in India there is no way of classifying an individual by the dress he wears. An industrialist, say a textile tycoon, may be dressed exactly like a retail fruit seller. Again, a scholar of Sanskrit, English, Greek and Latin might look like the humble priest of an old impoverished temple. How was I to discover and portray the common denomination in this medley of characters, dresses, appearances and habits?

In the early days, I used to cram in as many figures as I could into a cartoon to represent the masses. Gradually I began to concentrate on fewer and fewer figures. These my readers came to accept as representative of the whole country. It would have been awfully anachronistic if I had attempted to prolong the presence of the Bharat Mata figure in my cartoons to symbolize the common people and their post-Independence turmoils. It would have been ridiculous, indeed, if Bharat Mata, with her crown and untied hair, holding our national flag, was seen hanging around in the background at a cabinet meeting, a glittering state banquet for a visiting foreign dignitary, or at the airport watching a worried minister dash off to Delhi. It would also not do to portray the common man in any manner one fancied, as many cartoonists did: sometimes as an old man in rags, sometimes as an emaciated individual and so on, bearing the legend 'The Common Man' on the hem of his clothes.

Eventually, I succeeded in reducing my symbol to one man: a man in a checked coat, whose bald head boasts only a wisp of white hair, and whose bristling moustache lends support to a bulbous nose, which in turn holds up an oversized pair of glasses. He has a permanent look of bewilderment on his face. He is ubiquitous. Today he is found hanging around a cabinet room where a high-powered meeting is in progress. Tomorrow he is among the slum dwellers listening to their woes, or marching along with protestors as they demand the abolition of the nuclear bomb. That, of course, does not preclude him from being present at a banquet hosted by the Prime Minister for a visiting foreign dignitary. This man has survived all sorts of domestic crises for forty years, long after the politicians who professed to protect him have disappeared. He is tough and durable. Like the mute millions of our country, he has not uttered a word in all the years he has been around. He is a silent, bewildered, and often bemused spectator of events which anyway are beyond his control.

Besides my usual 'big' cartoons, I started a series called *You Said It*. A single column cartoon appeared every day in the *Times of India,* in the right hand corner of the front page. The idea was to make it a free-wheeling comment on socio-economic and socio-political aspects, free of real political personalities or actual political events. The feature did not attempt any serious analysis but reflected, with a certain conscious irreverence, the general mood of the country as a whole. I expected this column to appeal to readers who were not too critical and who accepted their humdrum lot without a murmur. My taciturn Common Man, who was appearing off and on in my bigger cartoons in the company of Nehru and his cabinet ministers, came in handy for this purpose. The other characters I built around him in this single column cartoon were villagers, bureaucrats, ministers, crooked businessmen, economic experts, rebellious students, factory workers—in fact nearly every type, from every walk of life, as the occasion warranted. The column proved to be extremly popular. It has appeared every day for more than half a century, except on those all-too-brief occasions when I am on holiday!

Gathered in this volume is a selection from the cartoons I have done over the last few years. I am continually surprised to note that most of them are timeless in their relevance to any given moment in our history.

January 2005   *R.K. Laxman*

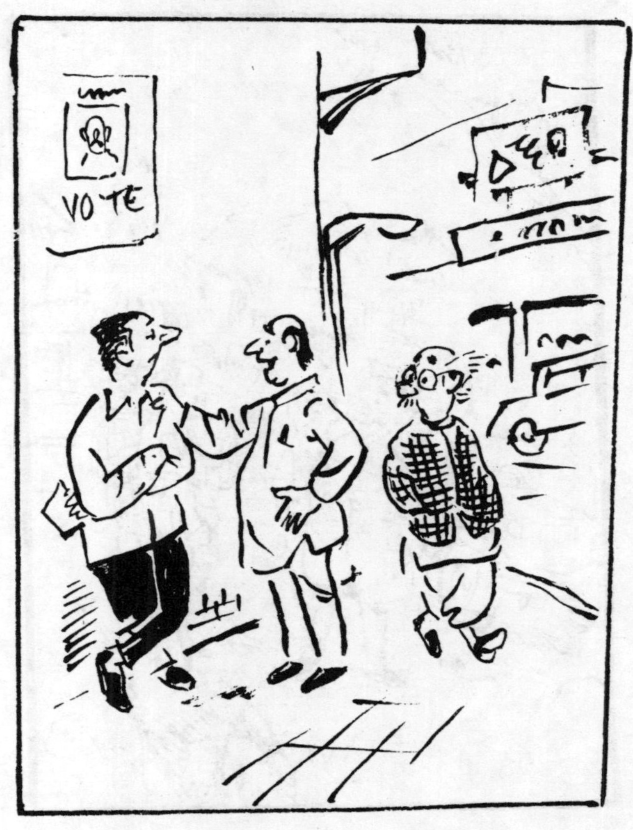

Maybe they all lack honesty, integrity and loyalty, and are greedy and corrupt. But that should not make you say you won't vote. It is highly undemocratic not to vote, whatever the reason, young man!

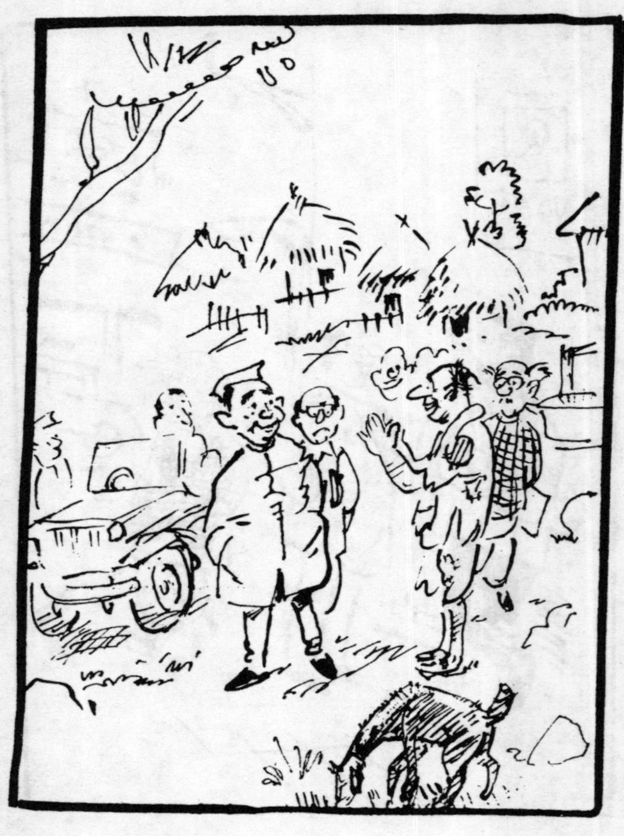

Thanks for asking, sir. There has been no change here since your last visit. But I'm glad to see that you look very healthy, happy and carefree.

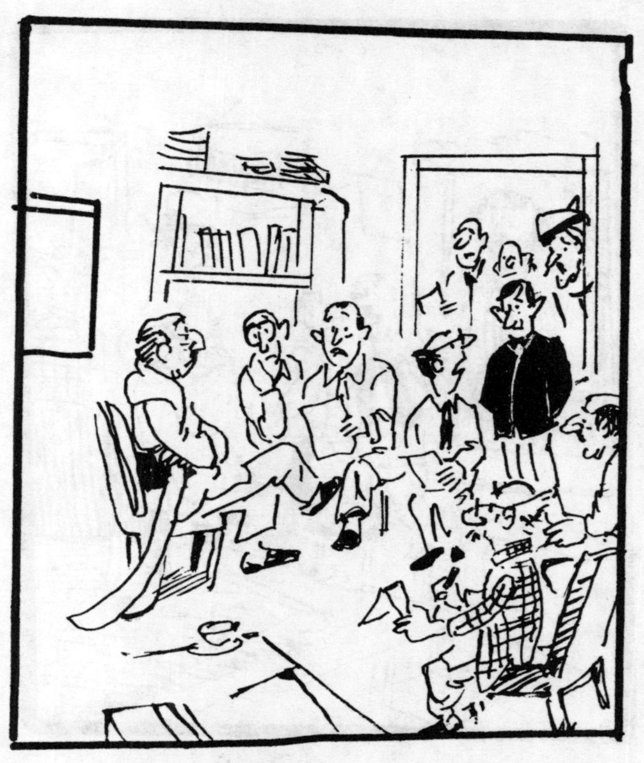

Why did he call this press conference in such a hurry? For anything we ask, he says 'No comments' or 'I am not aware of it' and so on!

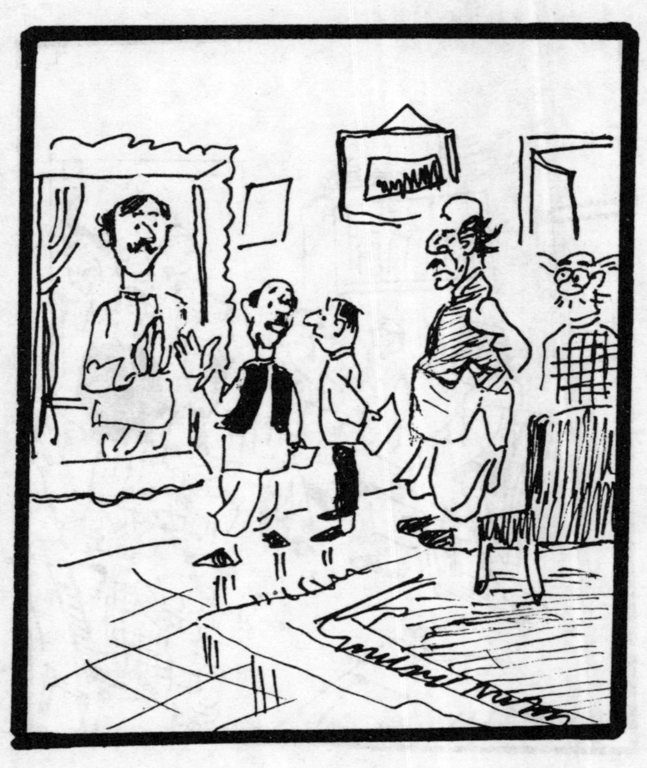

An old portrait of his. He wants it to be used in the posters for his next election campaign.

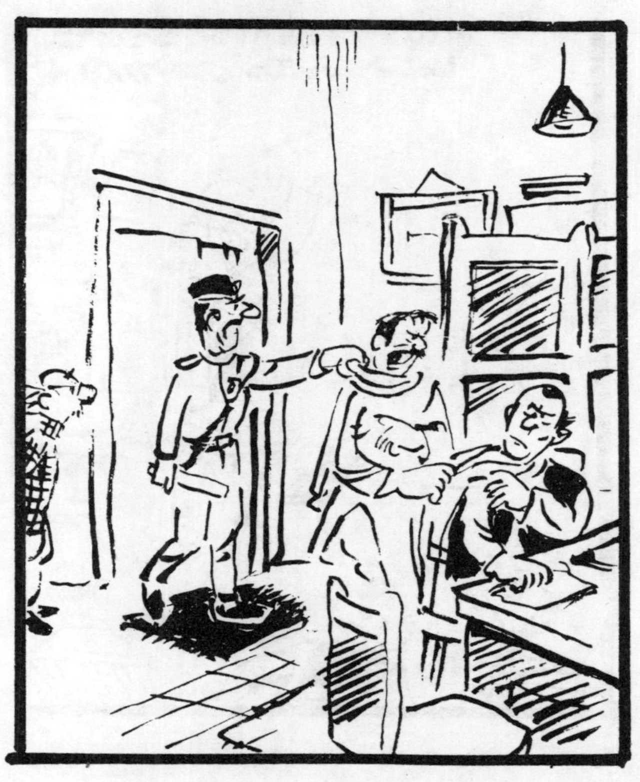

Ask him to lay off! He may be your security guard, but he has no business to protect you in our party infighting!

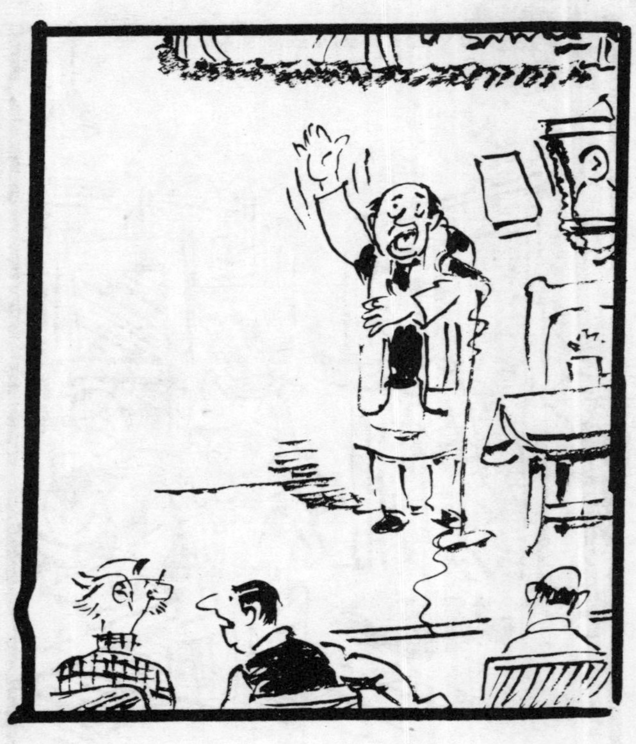

Formerly he just used to recite poems composed by him. Now he has started singing in the middle of his speeches!

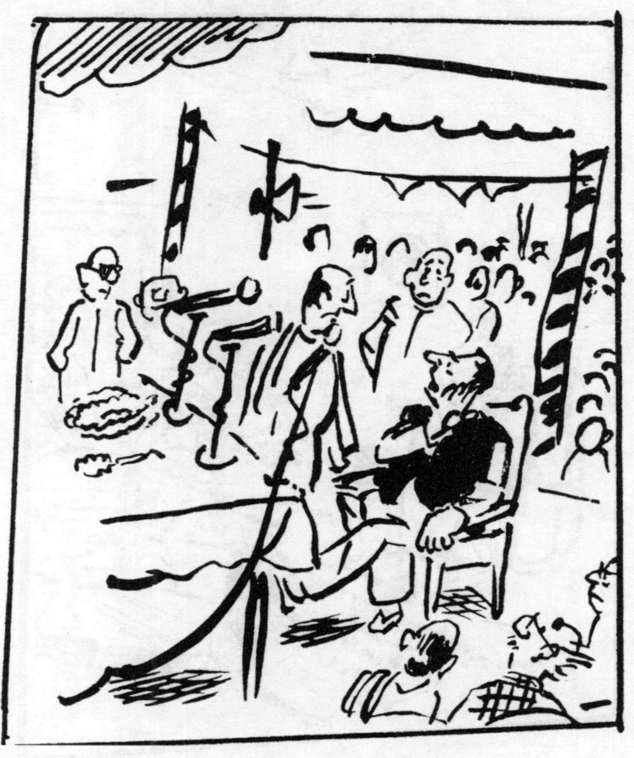

Don't keep repeating that you are innocent so frequently.
So far nobody suspects you of any scam.

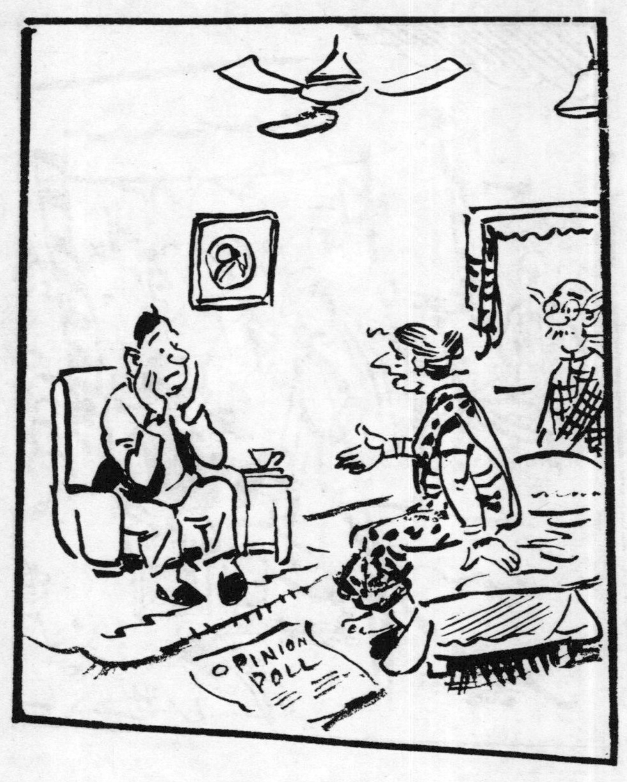

You politicians will never be happy! Look at the brighter side. If you fail to win, then you don't have to bother about fulfilling your election promises. Think of that!

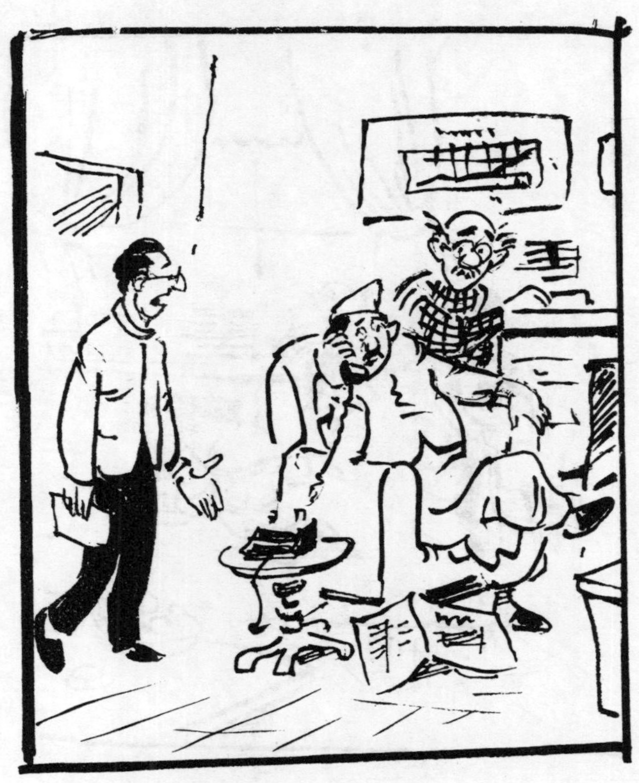

Don't use this phone, sir, for discussing poll strategy
with your party. You may get into trouble for violating
model code of conduct rules. This instrument belongs
to the government.

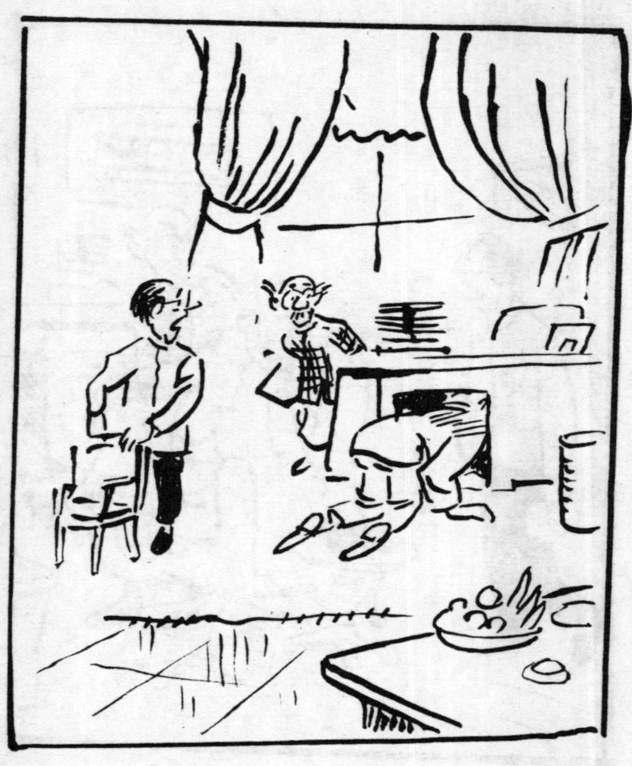

No need to look in there, sir. We searched the room thoroughly. There are no hidden cameras or tape recorders. You can invite your friends safely!

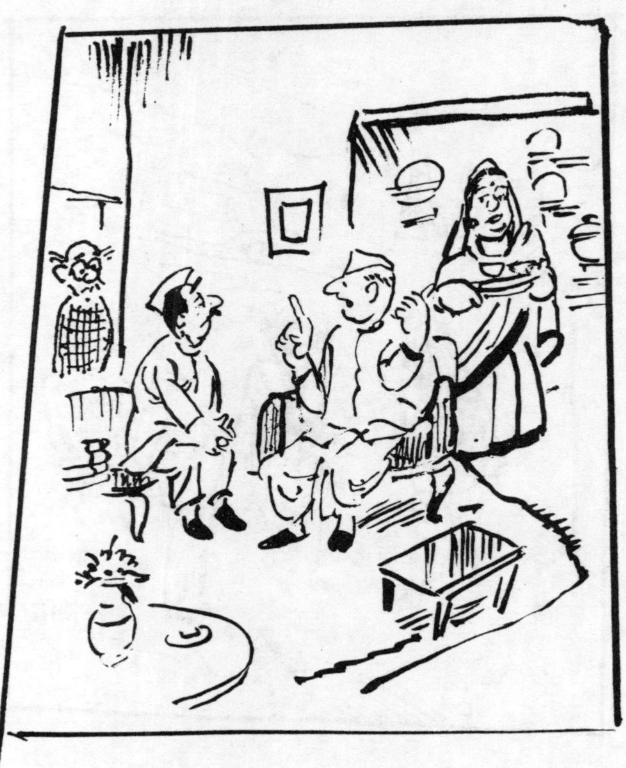

The party has unanimously decided not to let you stand for the elections but has requested your wife to contest, as woman power is on the rise. You have to take care of the kitchen etc. from now on!

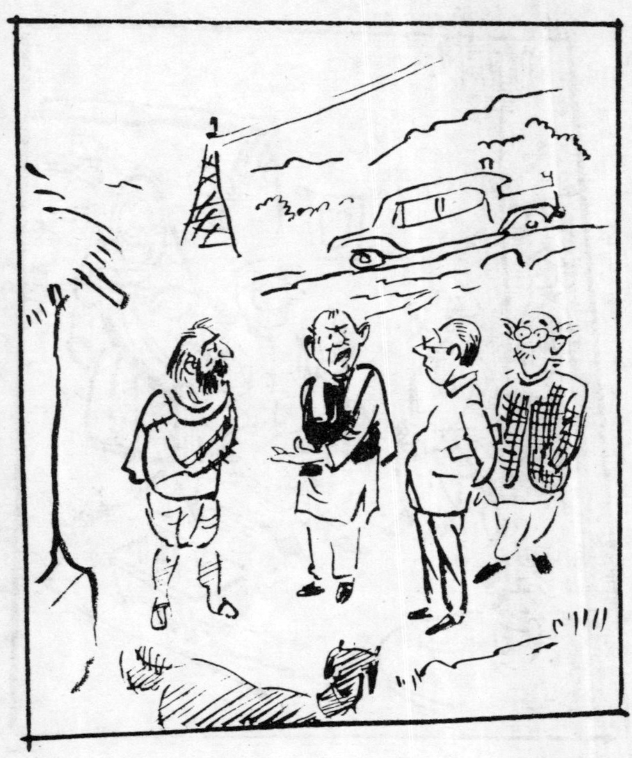

What's the matter with these people? I gave him all the good news—that Sensex is soaring, the stock market is booming, the economy is fine and that we won the match against Australia. Still he is grumbling and complaining!

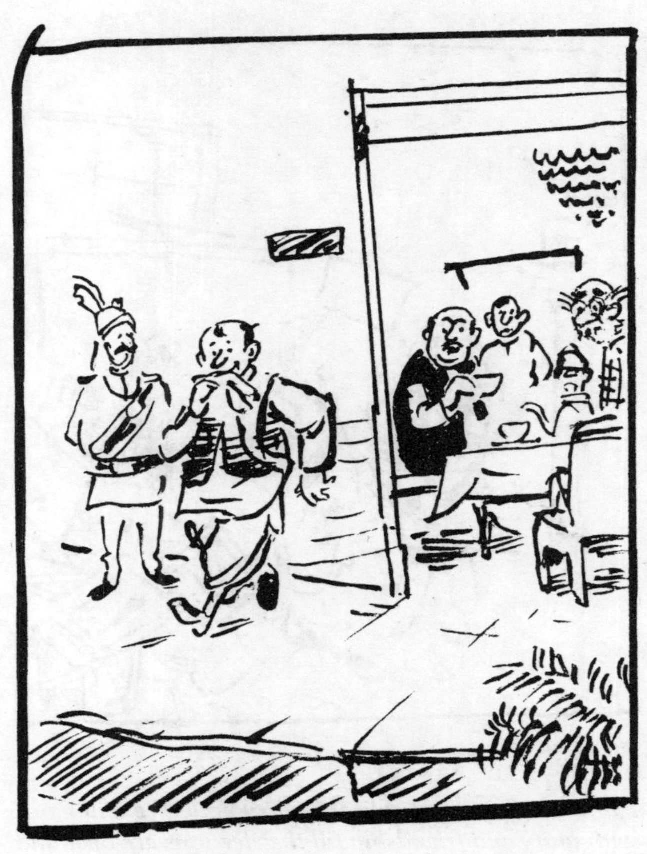

Look at that! I invited him for a cup of tea to discuss
the political alliance, the coming polls etc. He came,
gulped down the tea and scooted away!

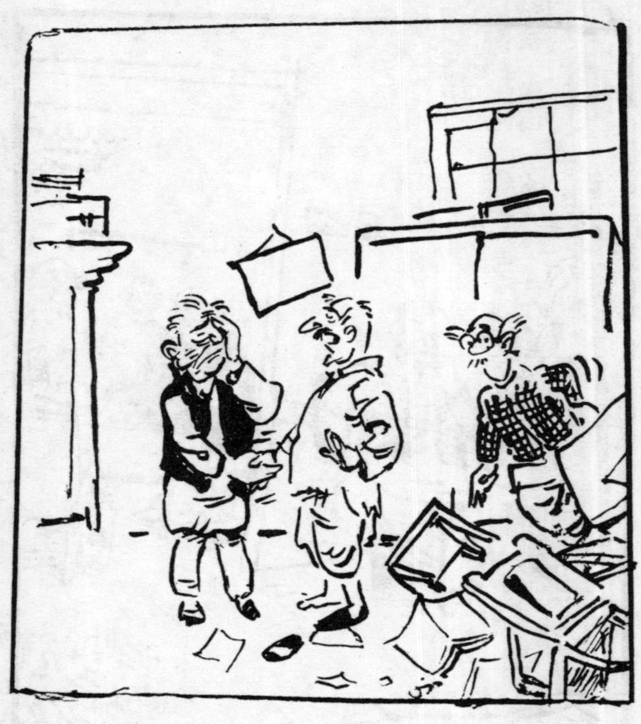

Fair enough, do not split the party now. We will work with unity and friendship till the elections are over and then split.

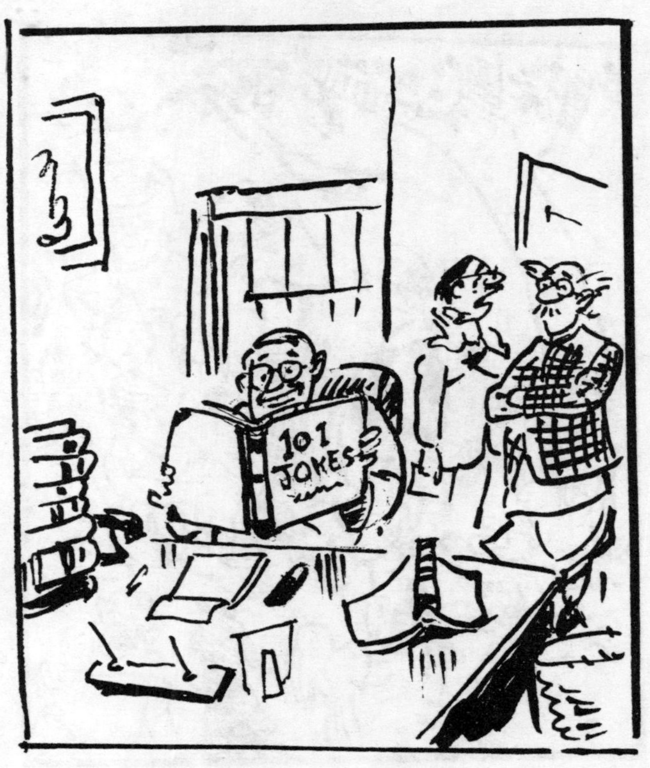

He feels his election speech is pretty dull and serious.
He wants to add some feel-good statements.

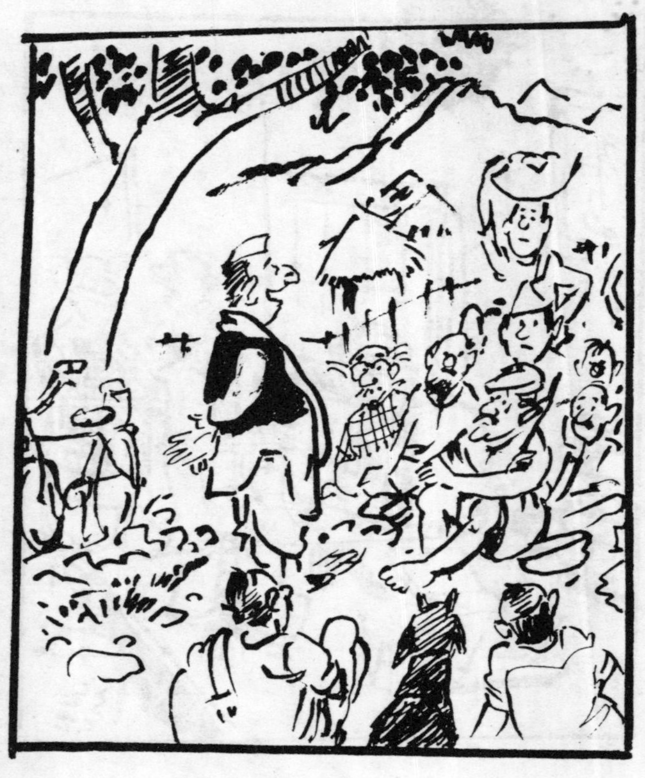

In the last five years of my term, I couldn't fulfil any of my promises because of our party's infighting, allegations of scam etc. Please vote us to power this time, and we will carry out all the old promises.

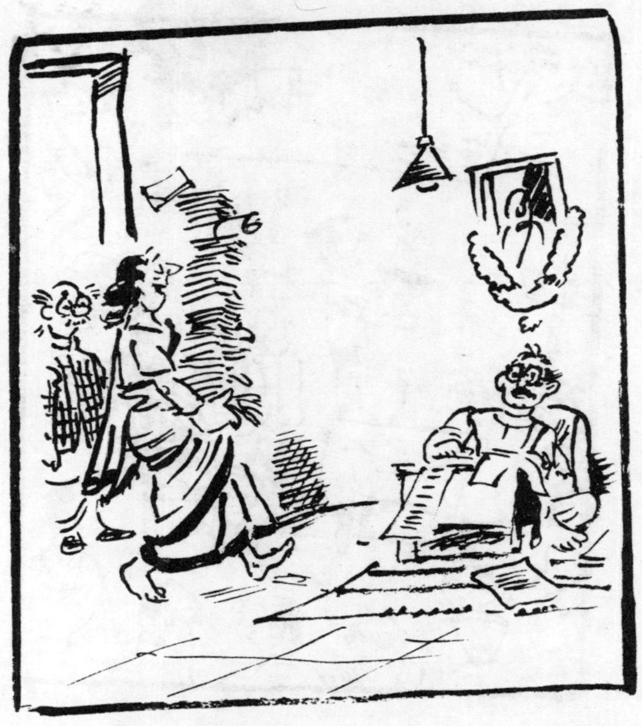

Here are all the election speeches you made during your long political career as CPI member, as BJP member, as Congressman etc. You can choose whichever you need for your campaign.

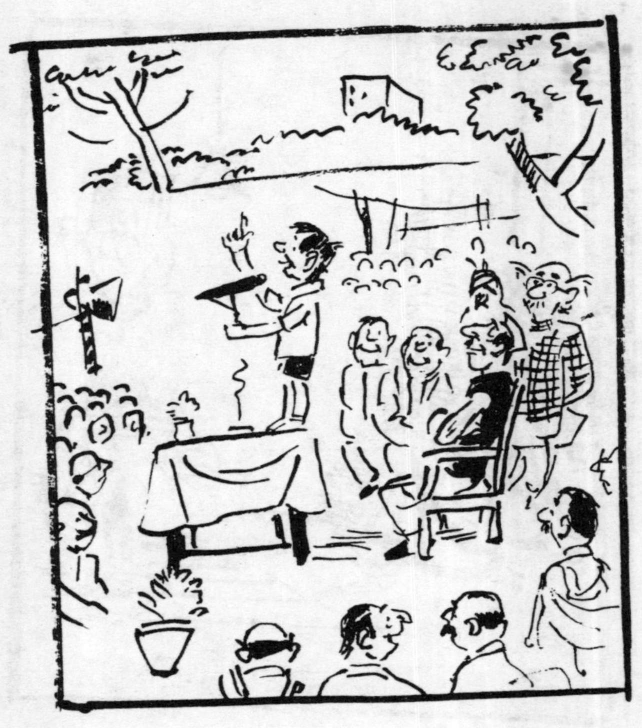

He has already started projecting his grandson as the future CM of the state.

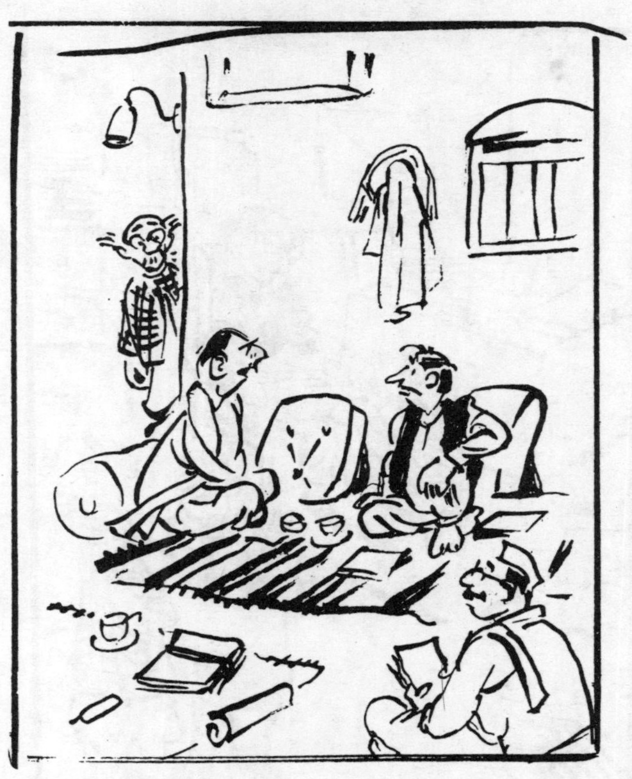

What's this I hear? You want to be gentle, dignified,
civil and friendly in your campaign! What's the idea—
you want us to win the election or lose it?

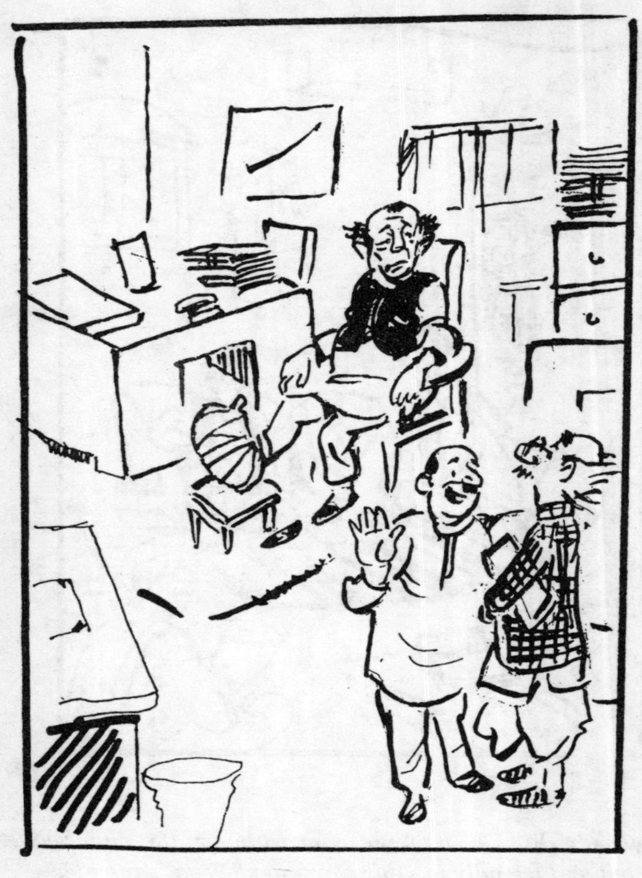

The function went off very well. He kick-started the election campaign but failed to see the table in front of him!

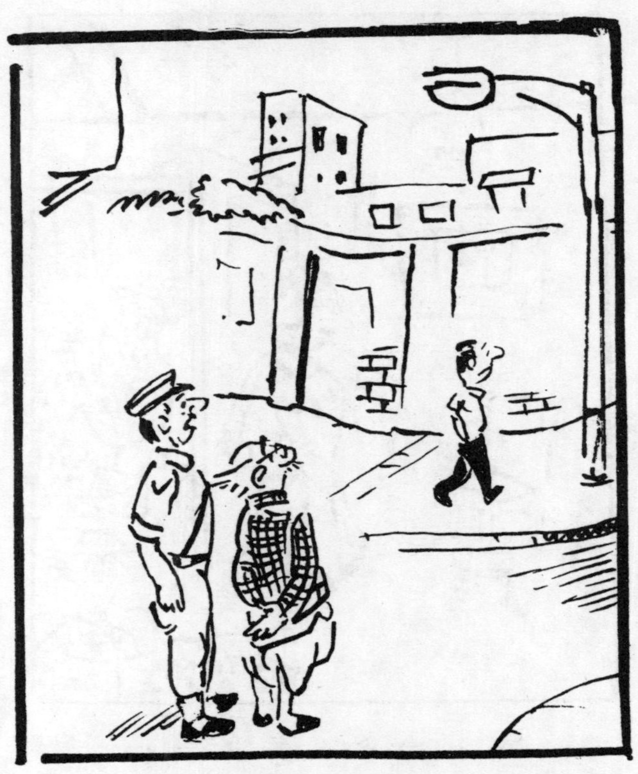

Why are so few people seen in the streets? Because most people in this town are involved in the stamp scam and are detained in police stations.

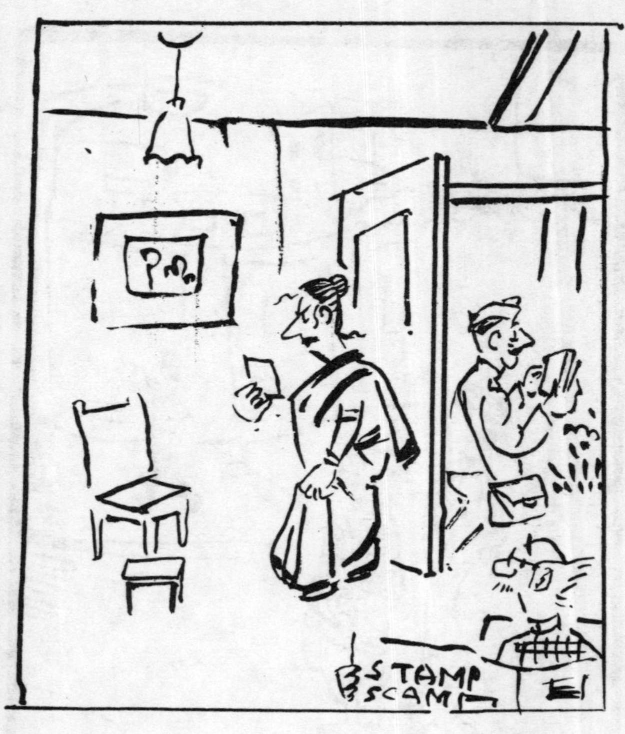

I knew this would happen. Instead of putting the picture on the stamp, this chap Telgi has put his own portrait!

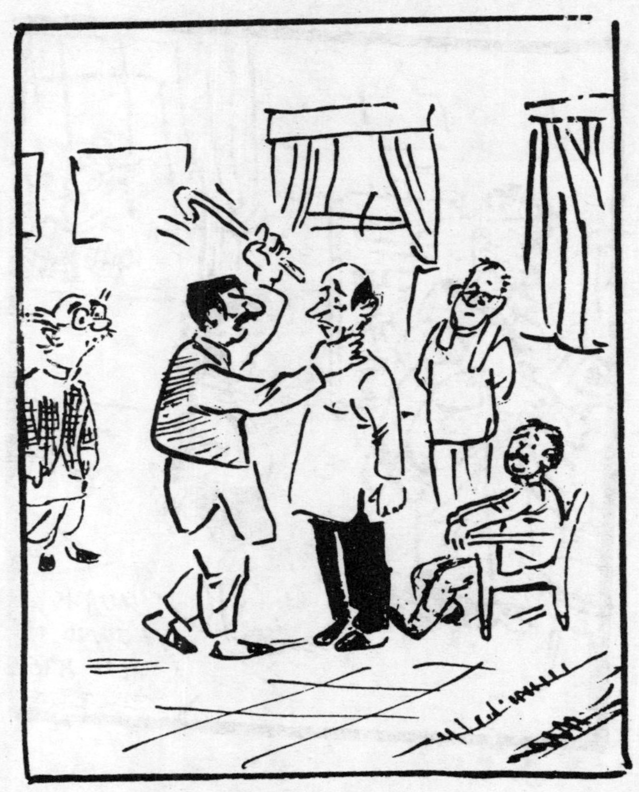

Don't you dare introduce me to your friends as the one involved in the stamp paper scam. What do you take me for? I'm involved in the cellphone scam. Remember, or else...!

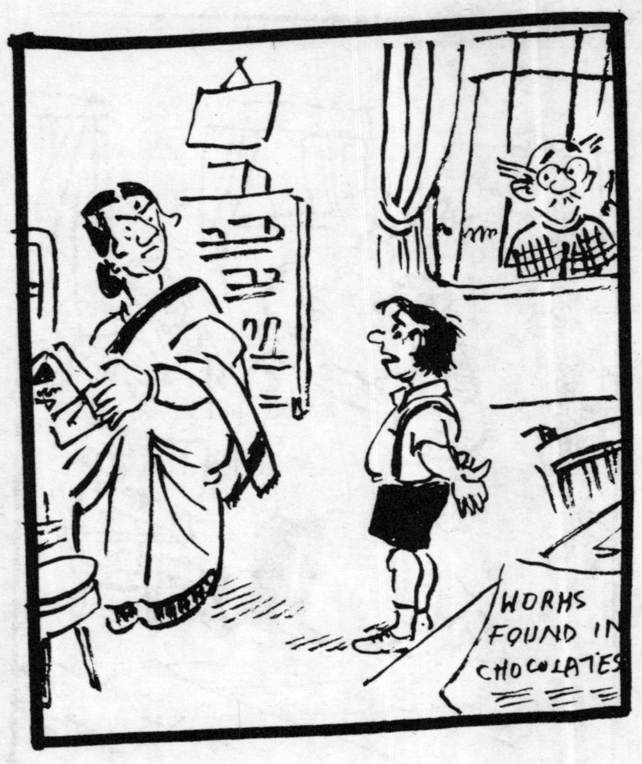

No, mother, I didn't take any chocolates. They must have walked away somewhere. They have life in them, you know!

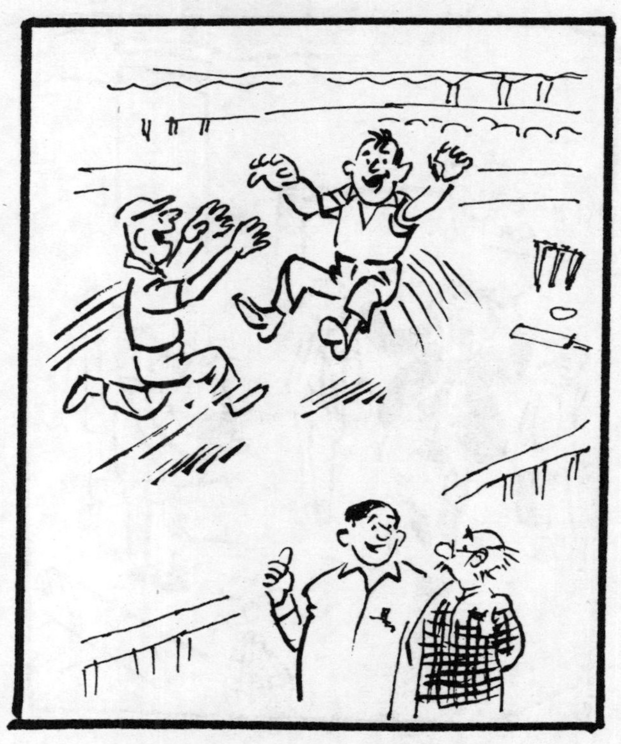

No, *they aren't practising cricket. They are rehearsing
expressing joy in the event of winning the match.*

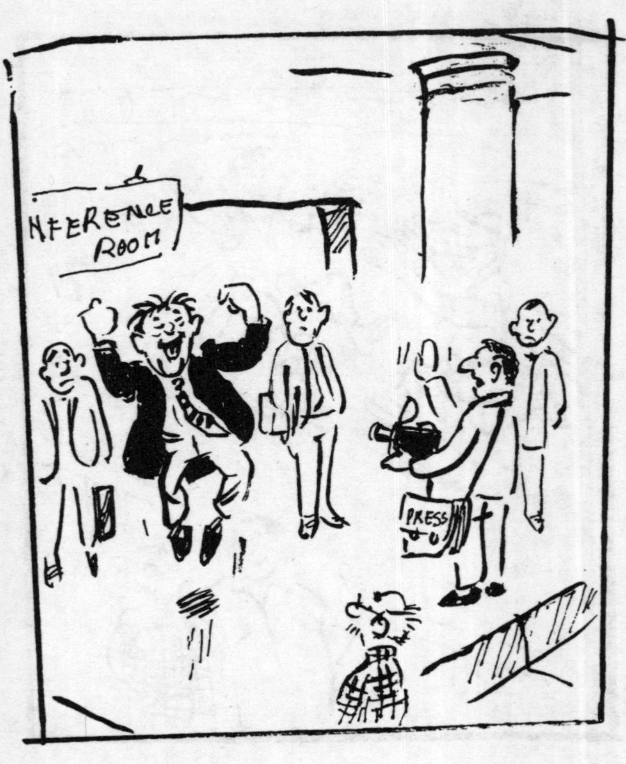

That is not necessary, sir. We know you are a famous cricket star. Just a gentle smile would do.

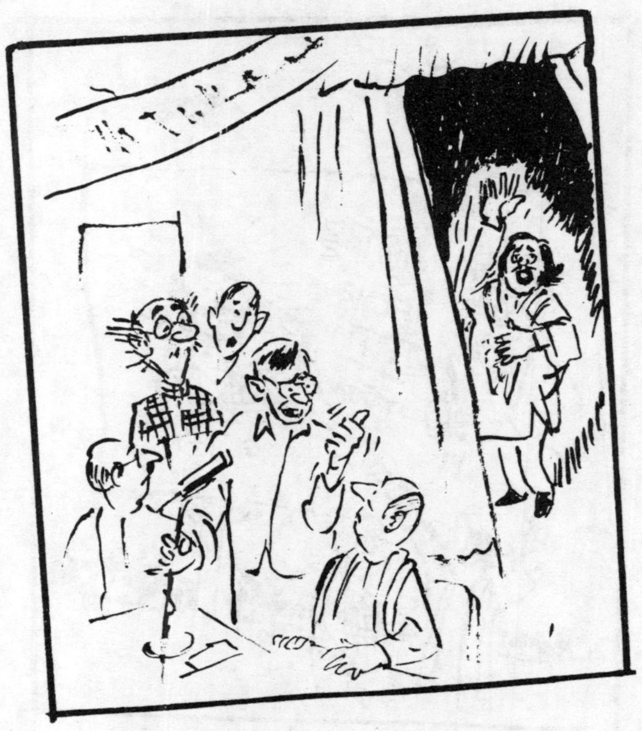

Can't we do something about the playback singer who joined our party? He starts singing every time I start my speech!

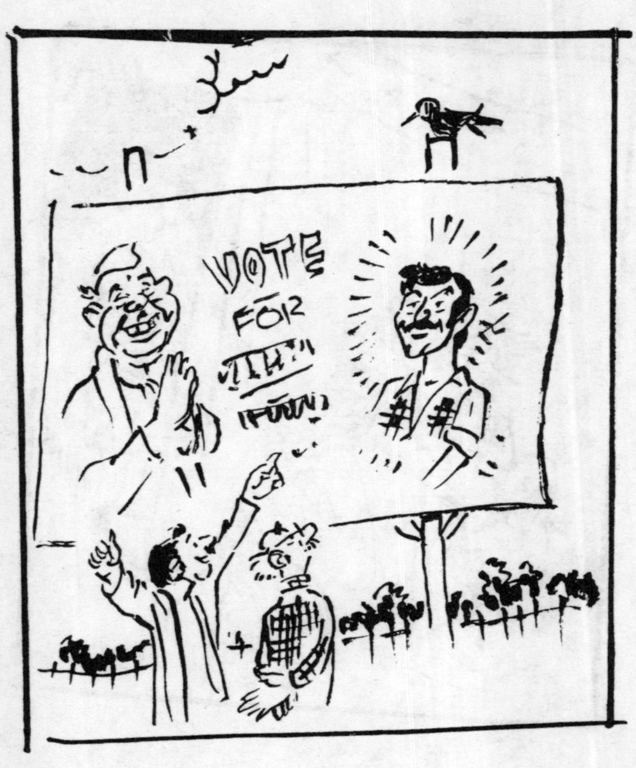

No, *that handsome fellow is a movie star campaigning for the one on this side!*

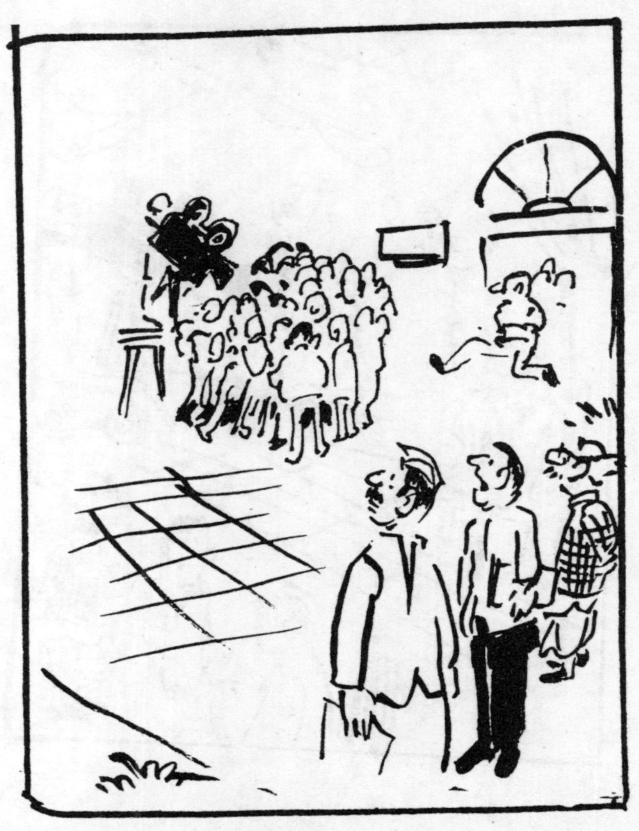

We should never have asked that movie star to campaign for you. The entire audience is crowding him for autographs and photographs, ignoring your presence!

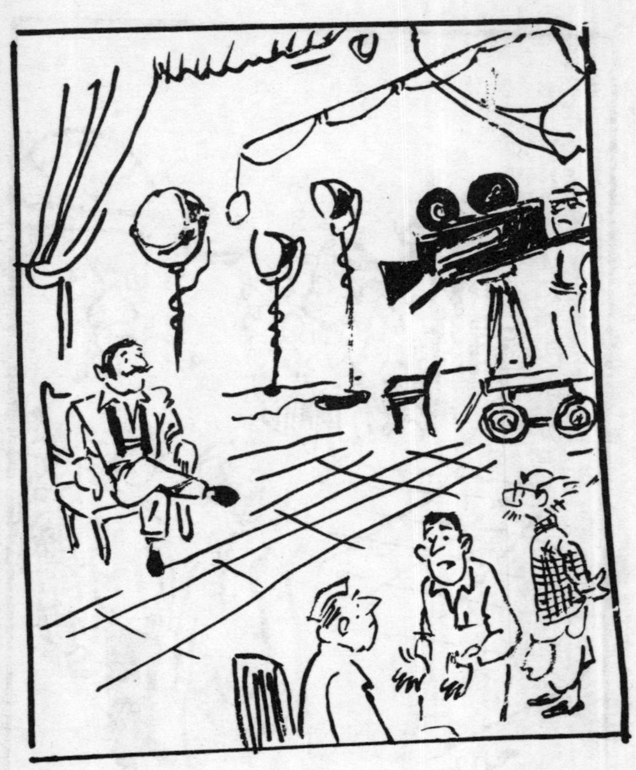

He is a famous singer, dancer and actor, sir. He has
already joined BJP, but he is prepared to defect to our
party if we double the amount he has received from
them. I think we should agree.

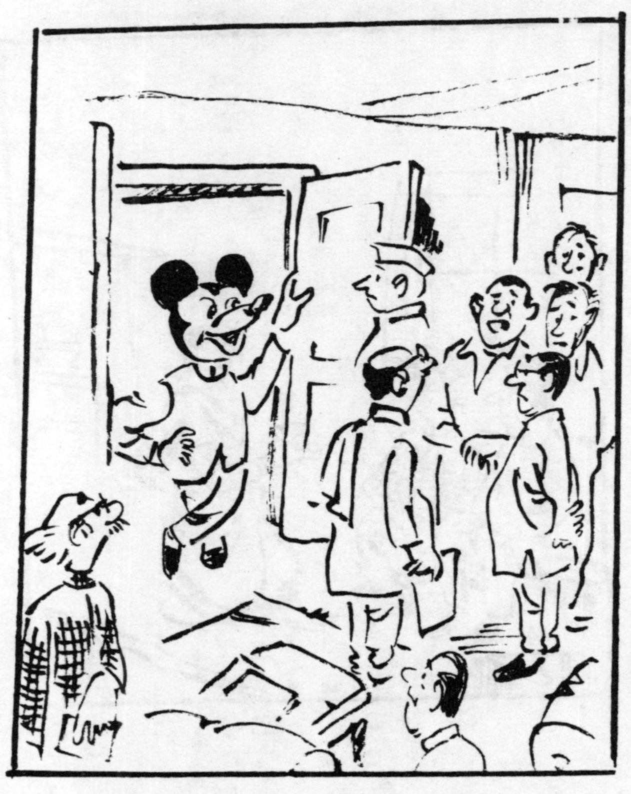

We have absolutely no objection to letting famous movie stars join our party and campaign for us. But the person should be of Indian origin!

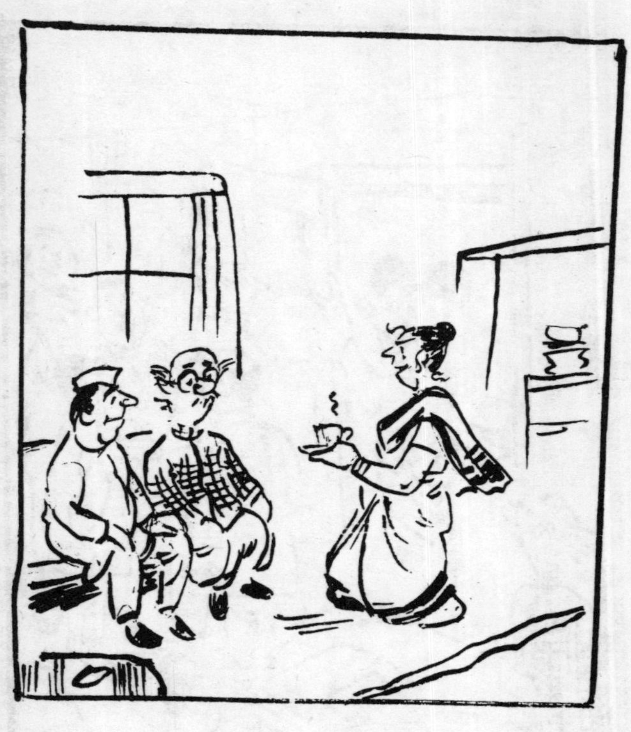

So many movie stars have entered politics. Why don't you politicians become movie stars? You act so well— expressing pity for the poor, horror at corruption, shock at crime and so on.

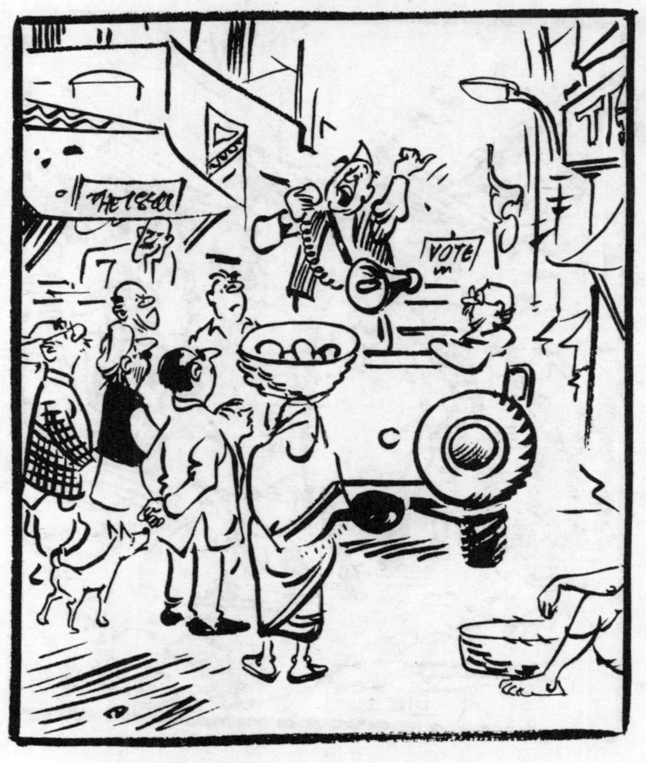

...if elected, I promise each adult a minimum of 100 roubles, I mean, rupees, a month...

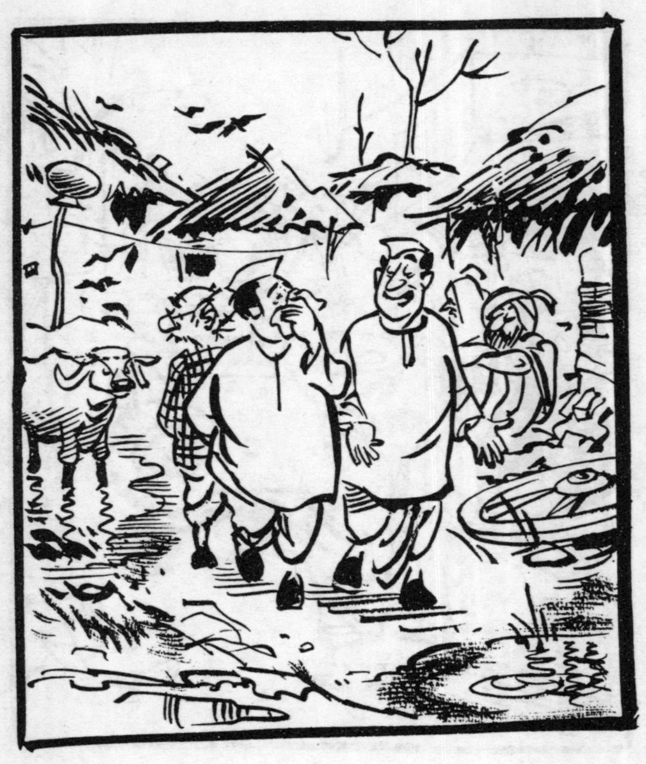

Utterly backward. No road, no water, no electricity. But I have always stood from this constituency in every election!

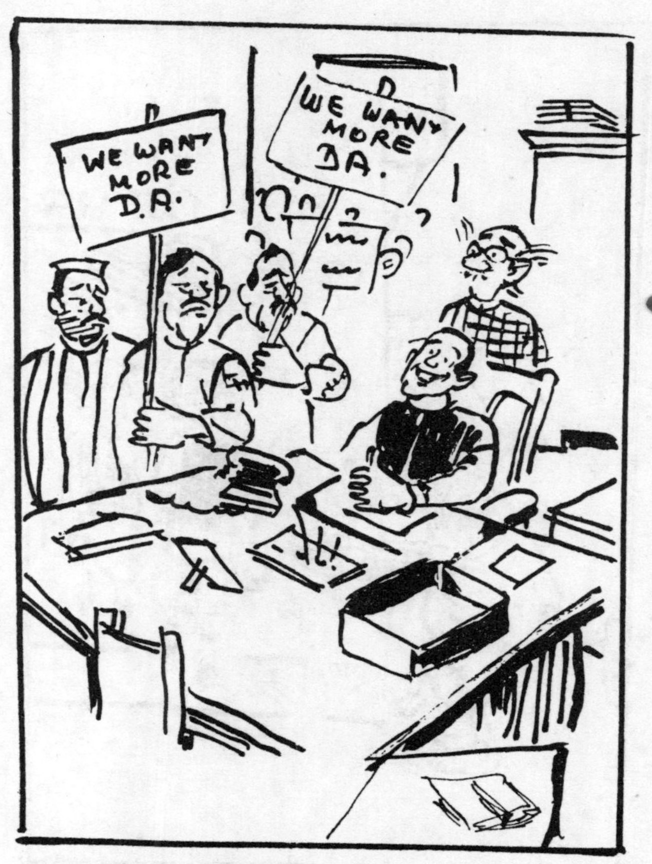

Don't you fellows read newspapers or listen to ministers speak? India is shining and the feel-good factor is spreading all over, and you chaps have come with good old demands!

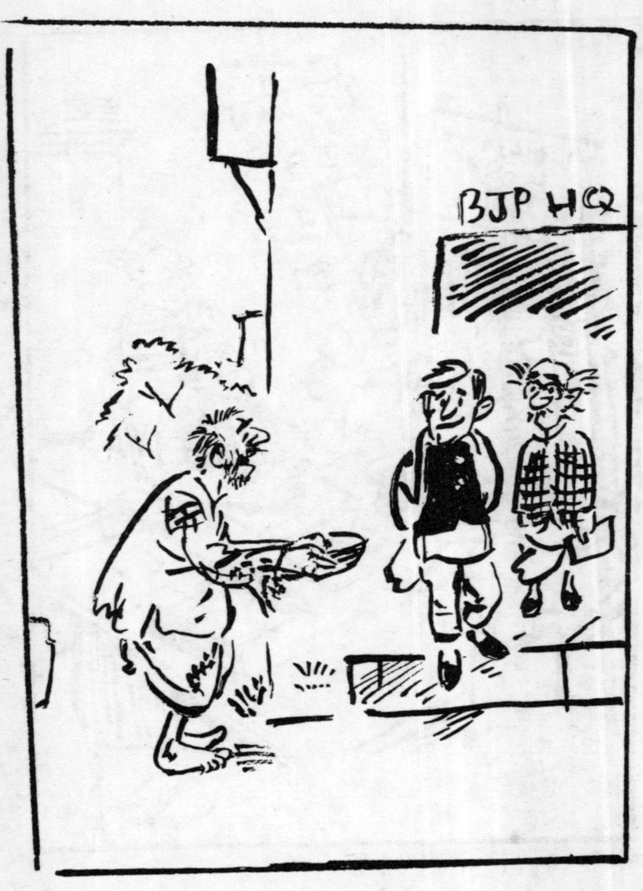

Thank you, I'm feeling good, all right. But if you drop a coin in this, I'll feel better, sir!

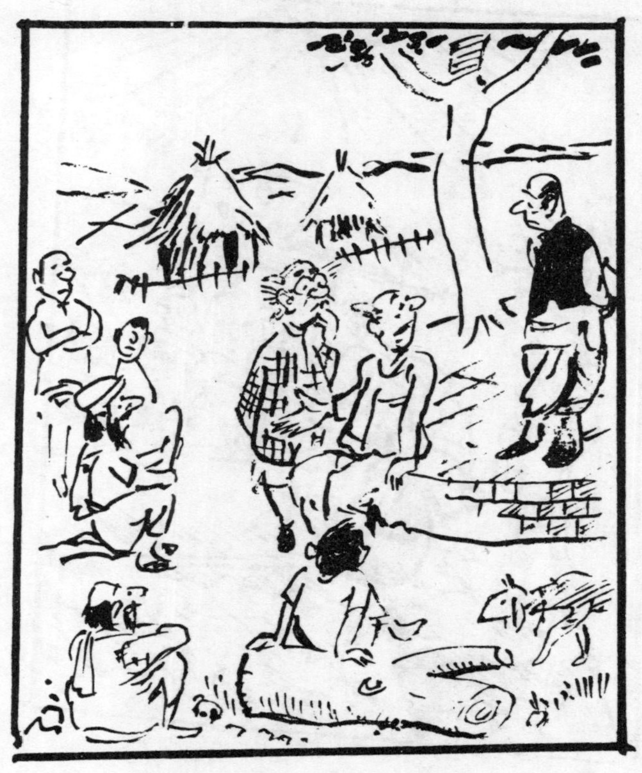

Stop making good old promises like giving food, water, removing poverty etc. Now start promising TVs, cellphones, computers, movie theatres etc. Remember, India is shining and everyone is feeling good!

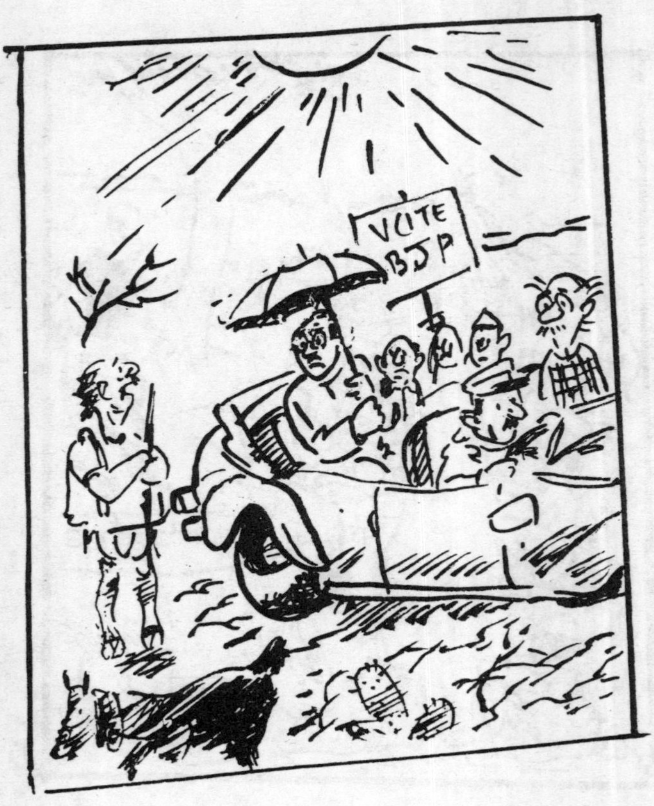

Thanks for making India shine! But can't you make it shine a little less? It has dried up our wells, ponds, rivers. We have no water to drink....!

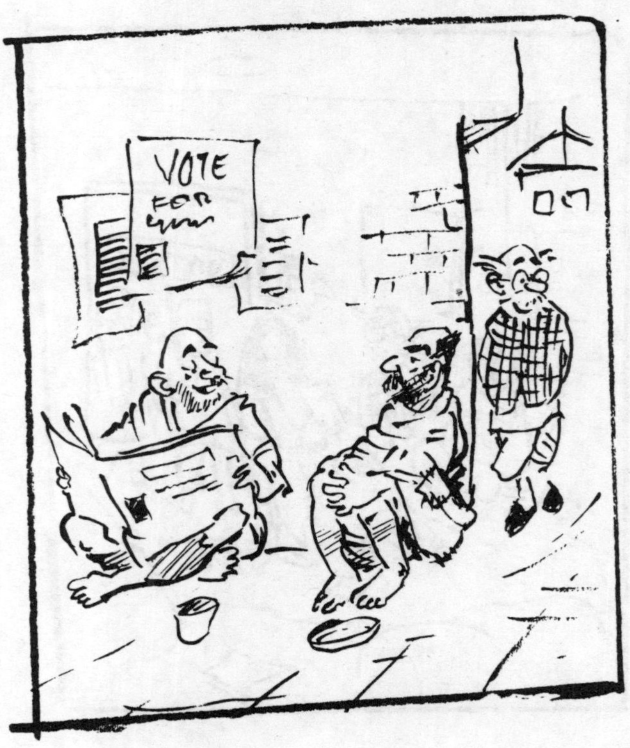

Want to feel good? Just have a look at the assets declared by politicians, ministers, movie stars—all in crores and lakhs, cars, estates. We are not a poor country, after all!

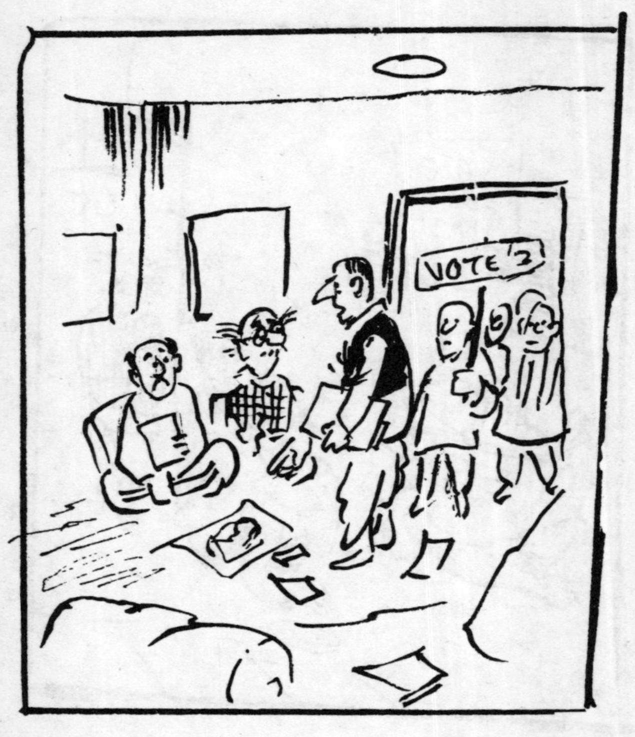

*I went there to campaign. But they wouldn't let me,
saying their village is shining and the people are feeling
good!*

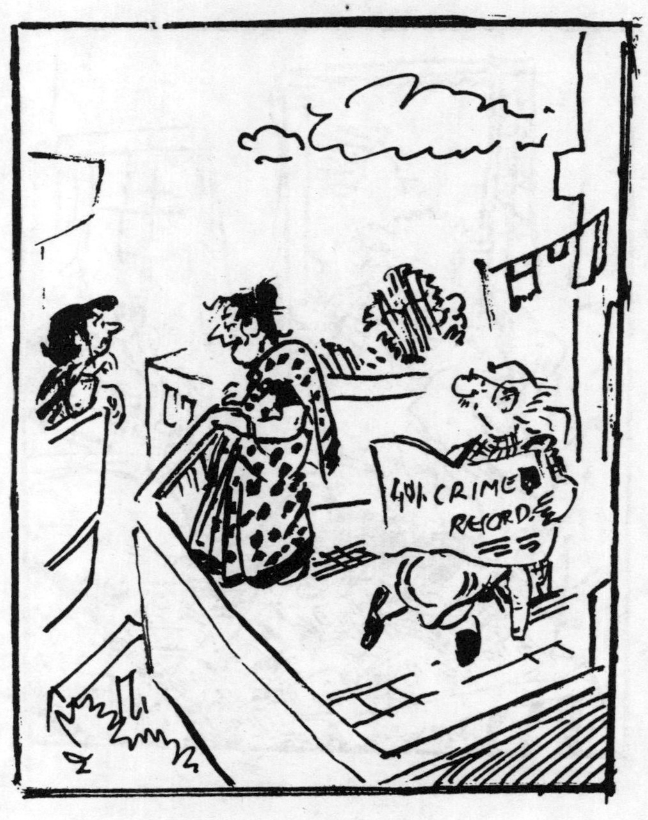

Yes, 40% of the candidates have criminal records.
Amazing why Veerappan did not stand for the elections!

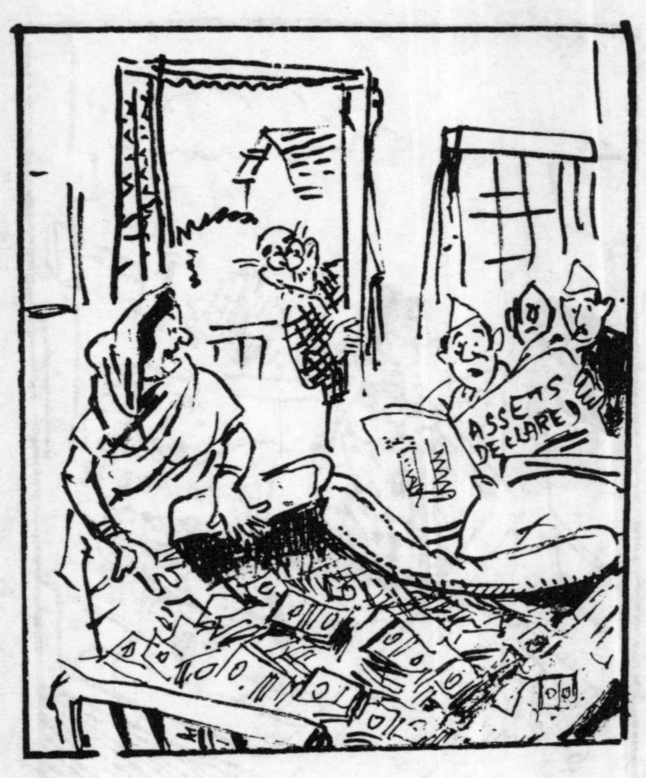

Good you forgot to mention these assets here under the bed!

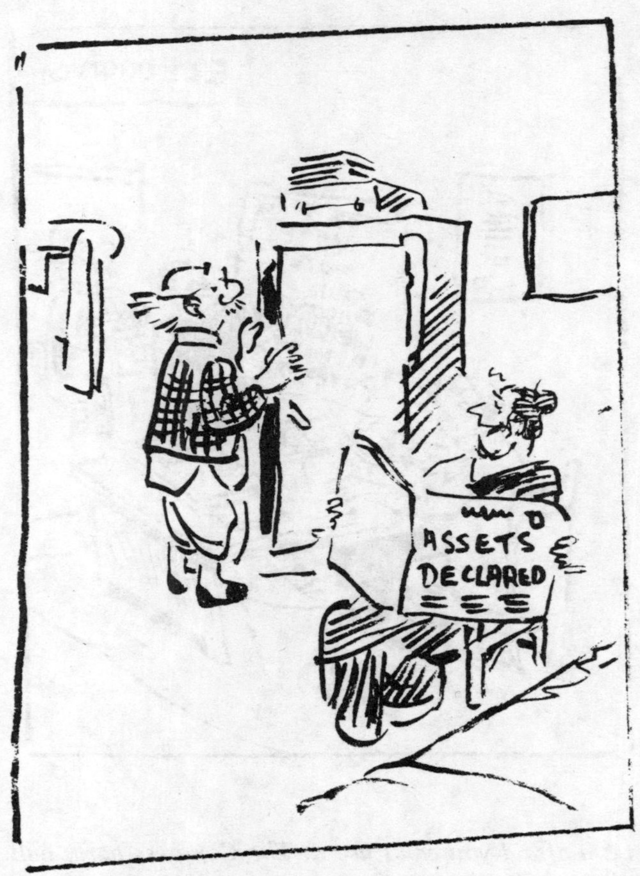

Who says they have not removed poverty? They have wiped out their own state of poverty! Ten crore in cash, bungalows, cars, acres of farmlands... that's what each of them has!

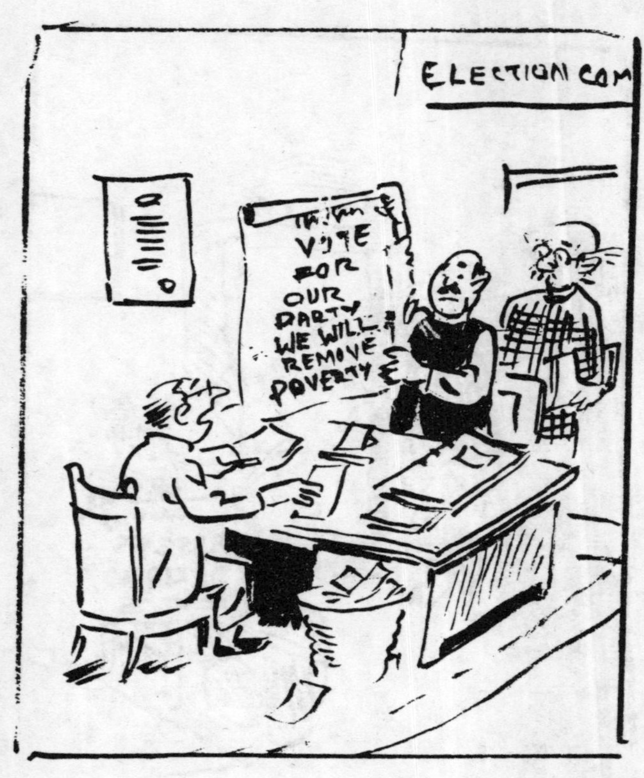

I am afraid you can't use it. The Congress party will object. It has been using it for years!

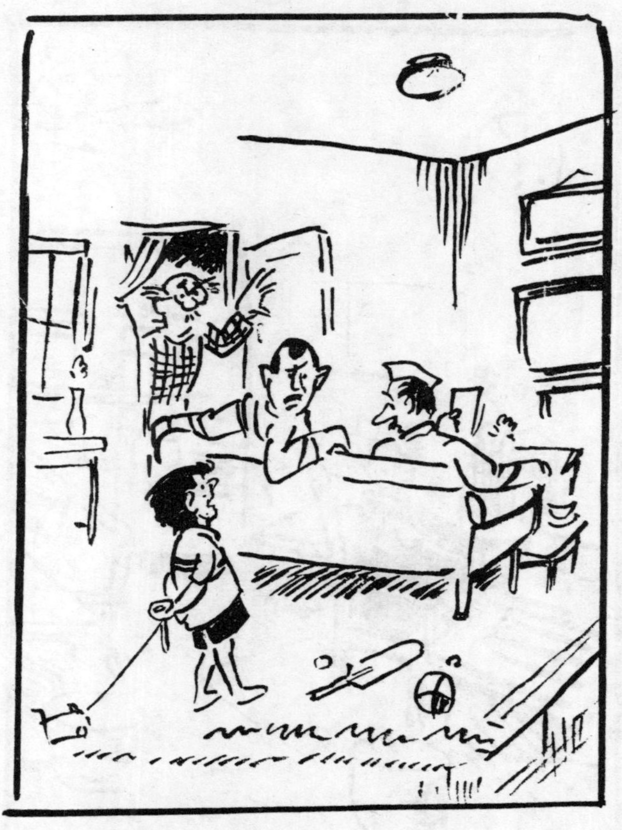

No, I told you, you can't join any political party! Things *have not come to that state yet!*

45

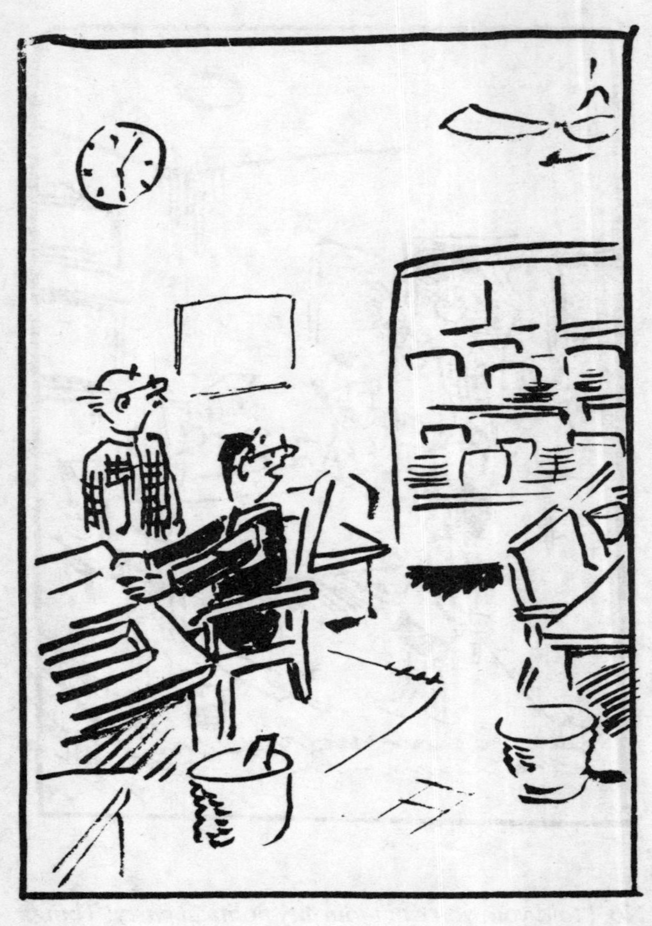

Why has no one turned up at the office today? Is a cricket match on somewhere in the world?

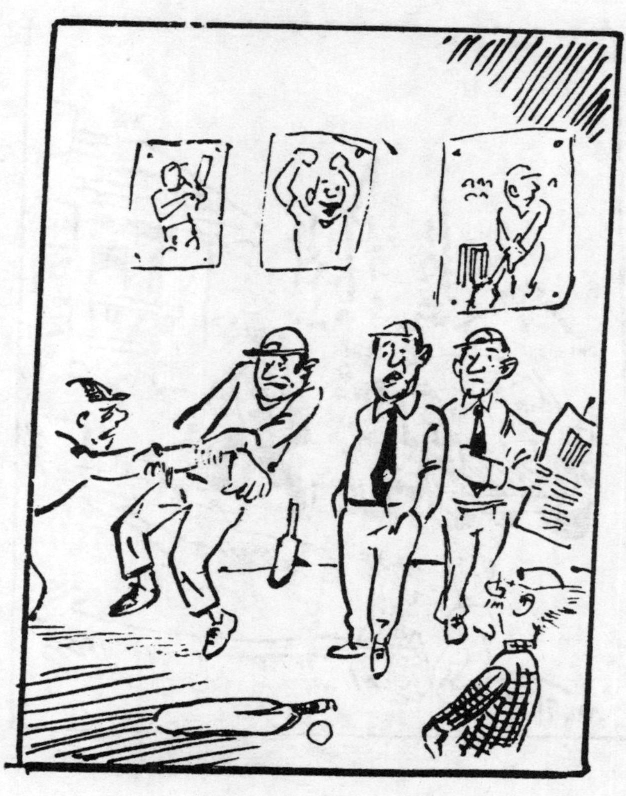

Selecting the team to go to Pakistan has become a tough job!

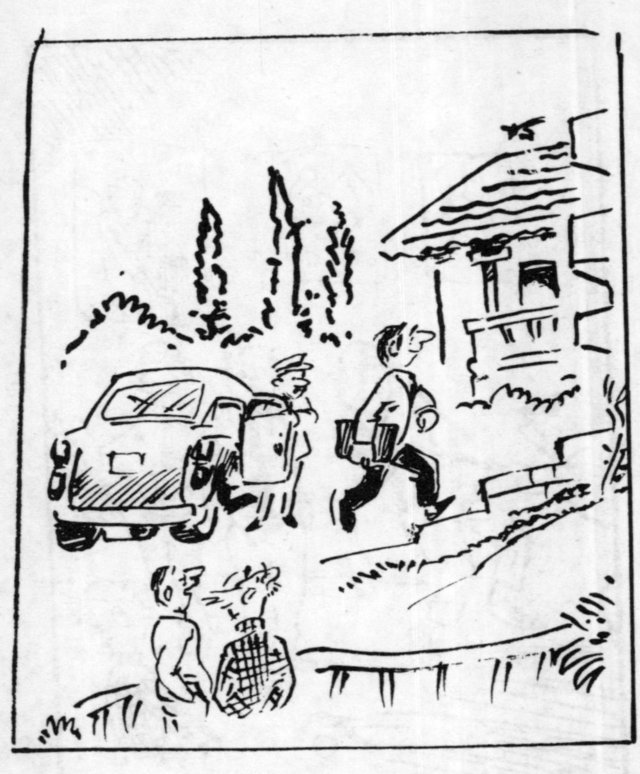

He became a millionaire by selling papers. No, not newspapers but exam question papers and stamp papers!

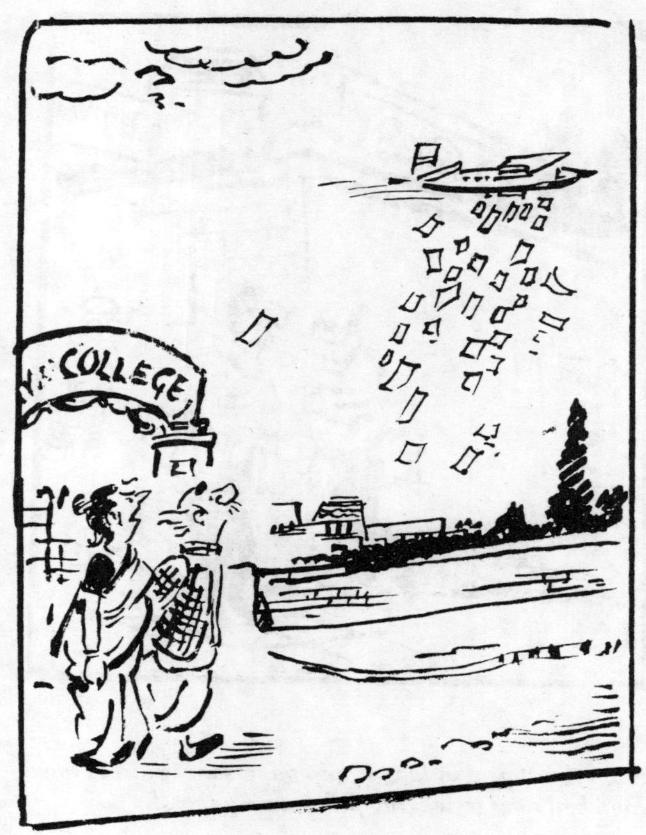

The chaps who are leaking out the exam papers are becoming bolder and bolder with the passing of each day!

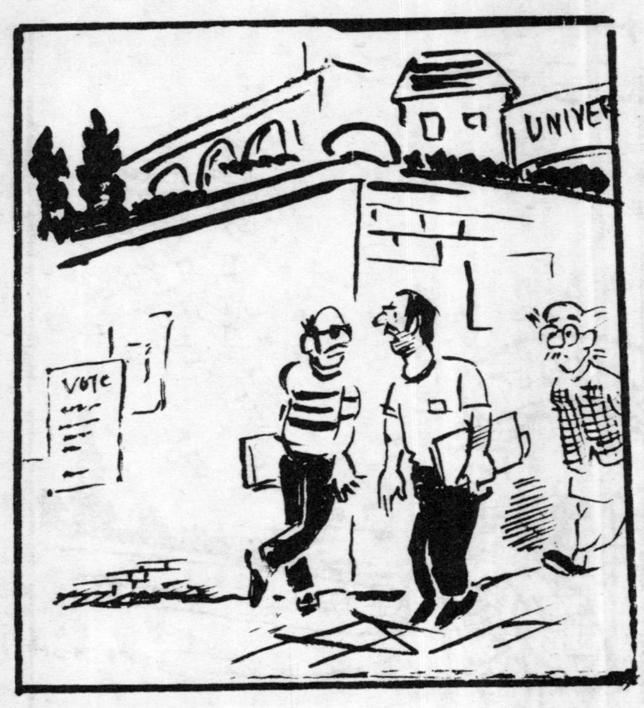

No, I don't deal in fake stamp papers any more. I have switched over to leaking fake exam papers!

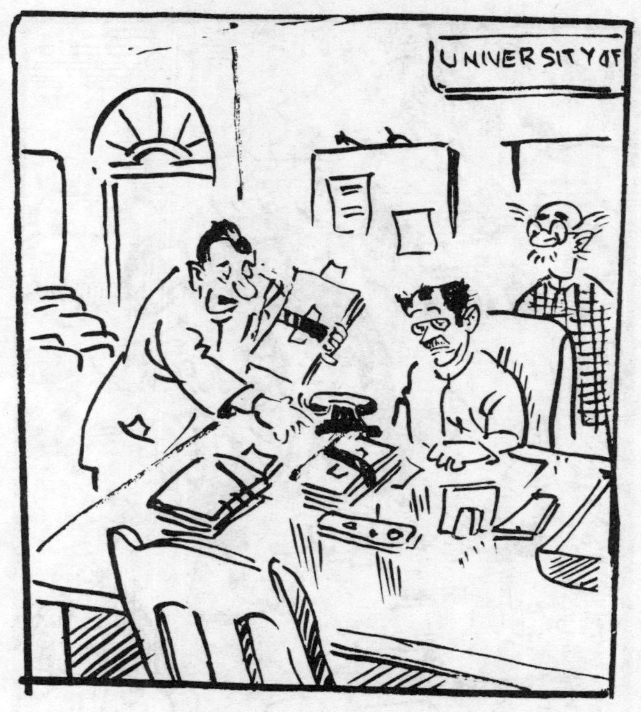

These question papers are for leaking and those for holding re-examination!

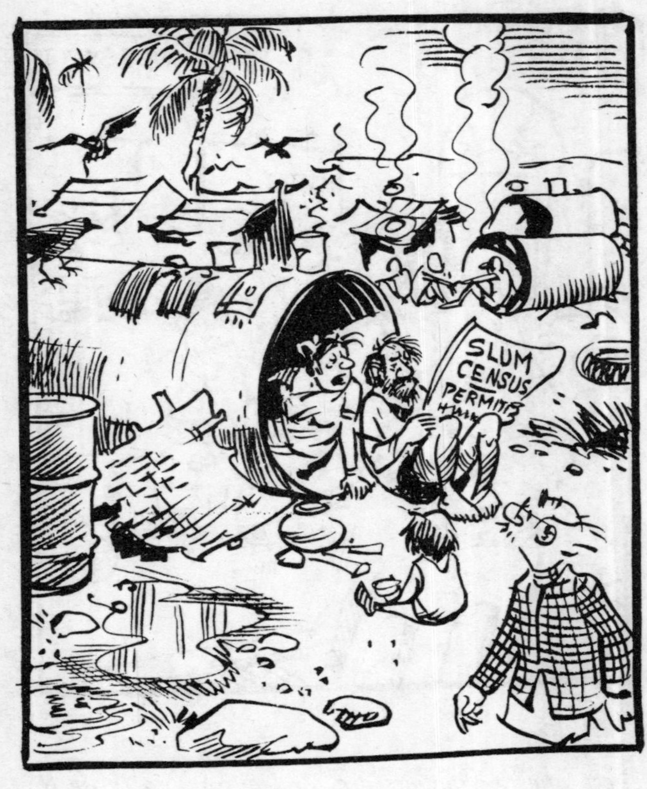

Get yourself a shave, put on some decent clothes and have a couple of photographs taken... Who knows they may come to our dwellings too to issue permits!

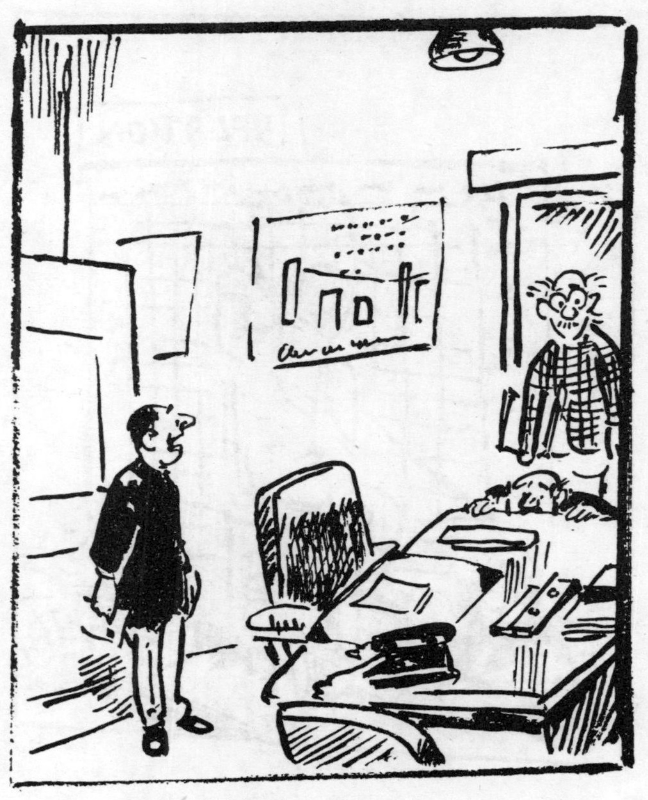

It's only the postman, sir, not a policeman!

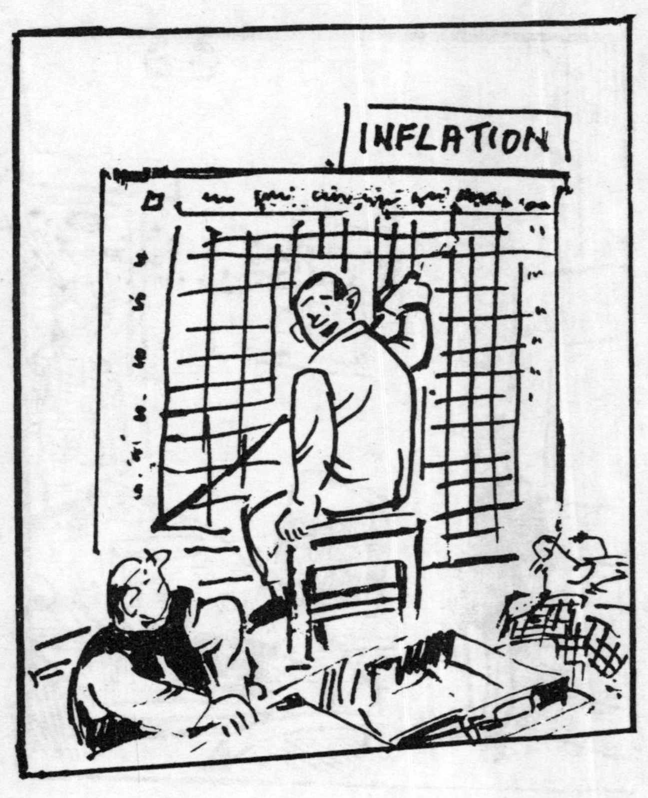

Shall I extend it further up to include the coming two days, sir? I am taking a couple of days off, you see!

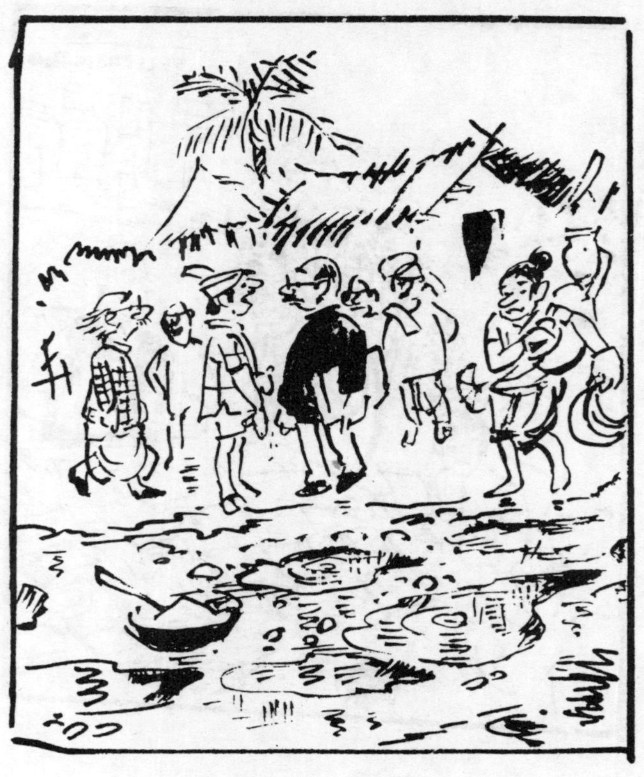

No, I didn't fill up the potholes, sir. The people here wouldn't let me. They use the rainwater collected in them as there is no proper water supply here!

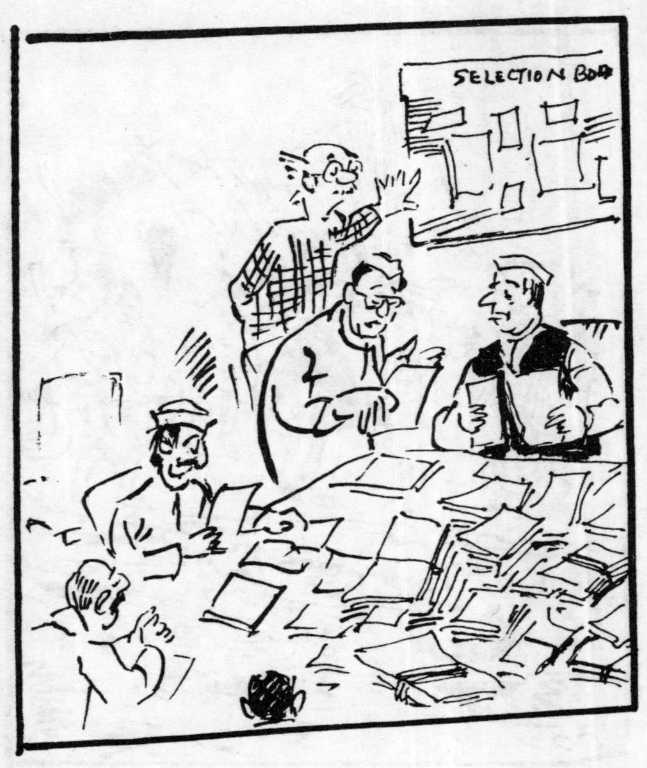

He is quite honest, sir. We can select him. Only two cases of scam against him.

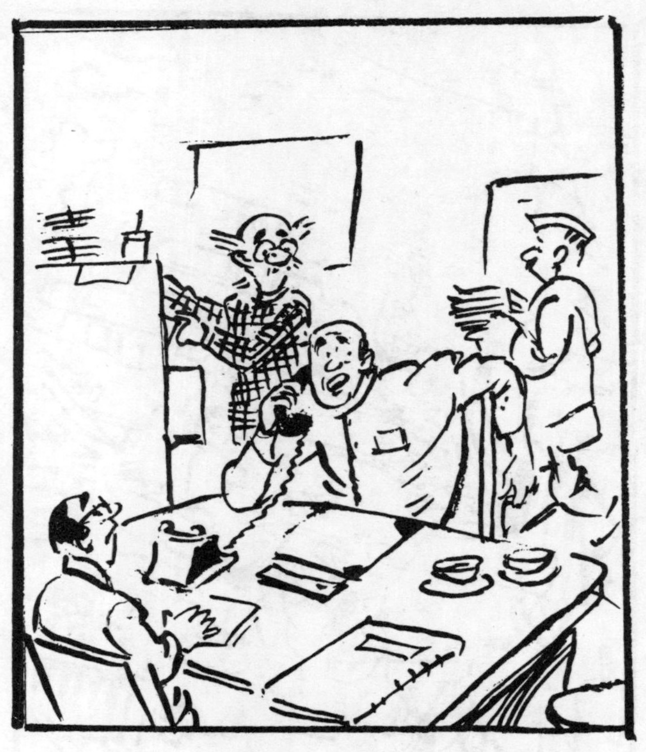

Which party do I belong to now? Congress... sorry, no, JD... sorry, it's BJP... did you get it? NCP...

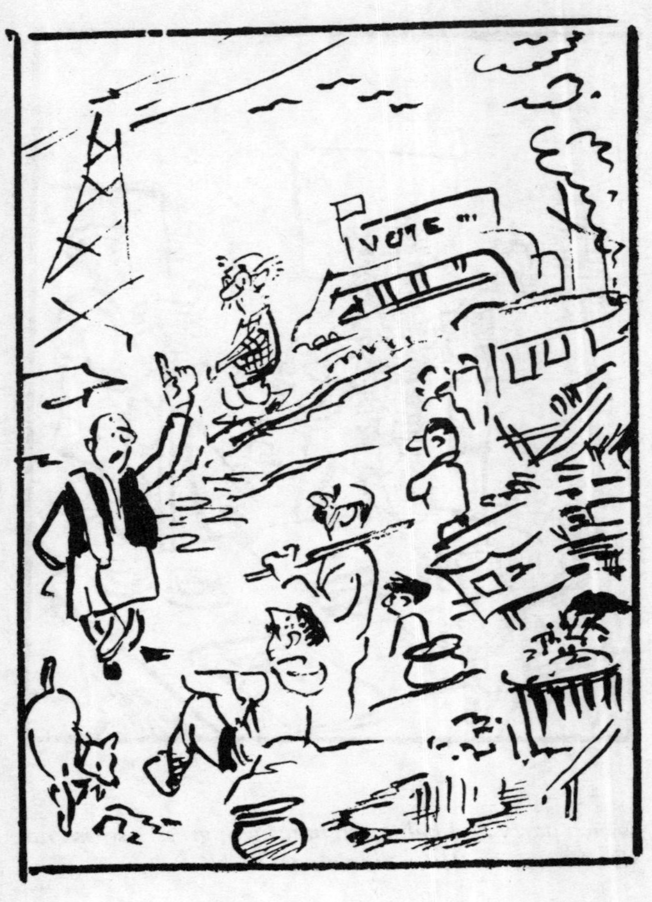

Give me your vote and I'll see to it that your slum is untouched and left as it is.

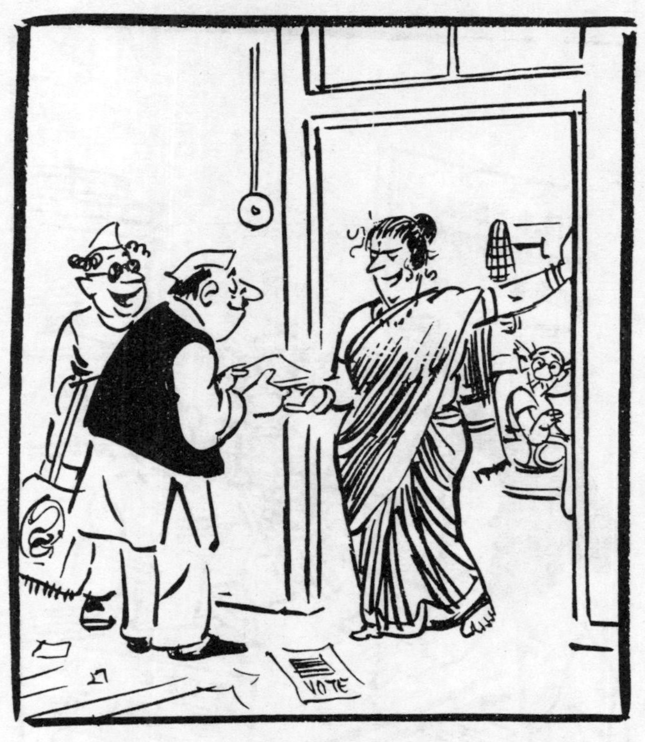

Certainly we will vote for you. So far we haven't said 'no' to anyone who has asked for it.

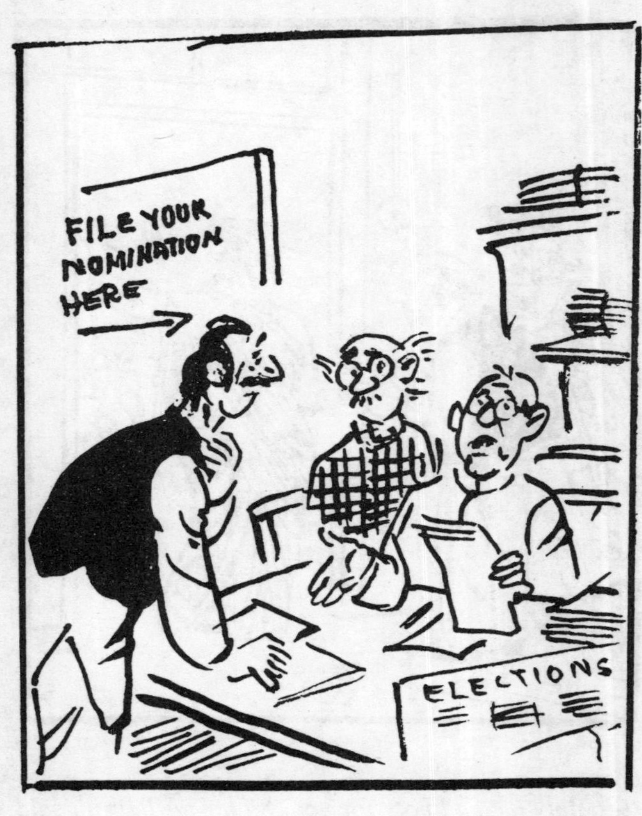

My criminal record? Sorry, I don't have any!

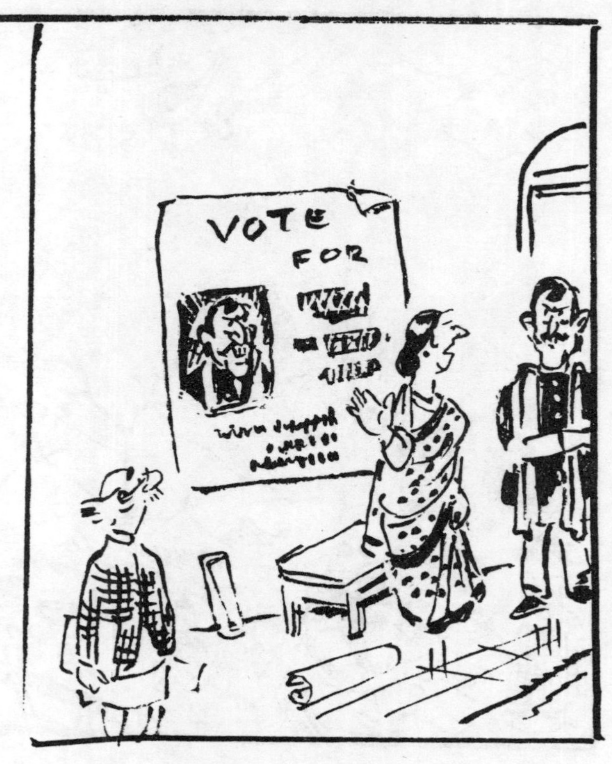

Surely you are not going to use that horrible photo of yours for your poll campaign! You will never get a vote with that!

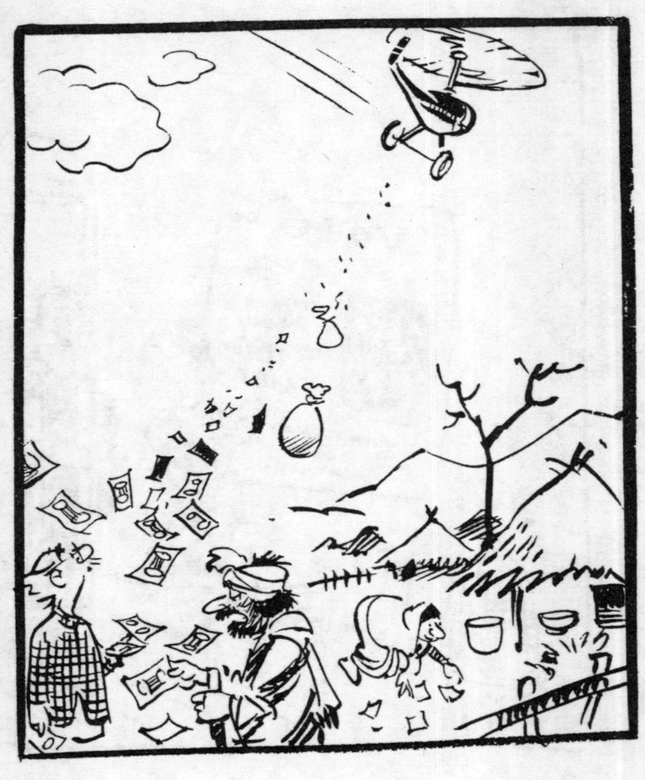

Election gimmick! Looks like they are pretty nervous this time!

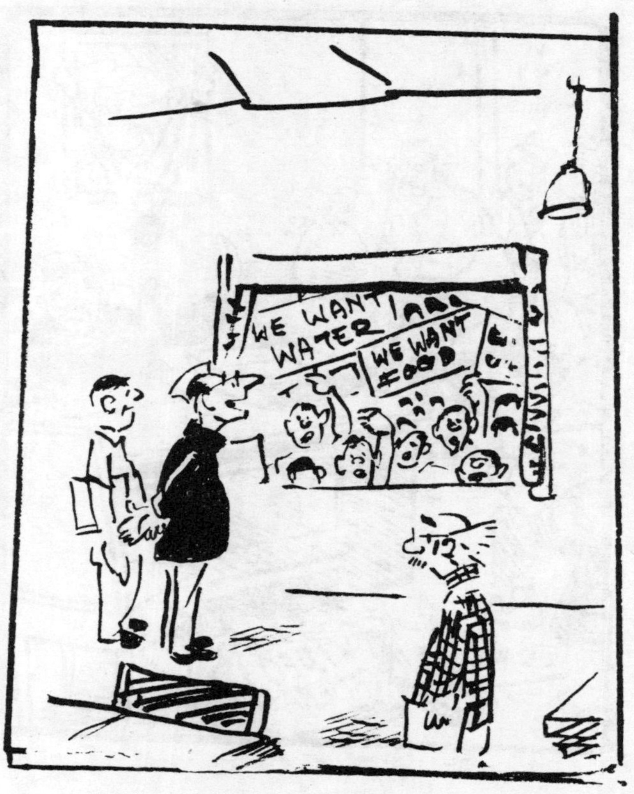

They have simplified our bother of drafting the manifesto for the coming polls. They are demanding food, water, shelter etc. We will promise them all that in our manifesto...

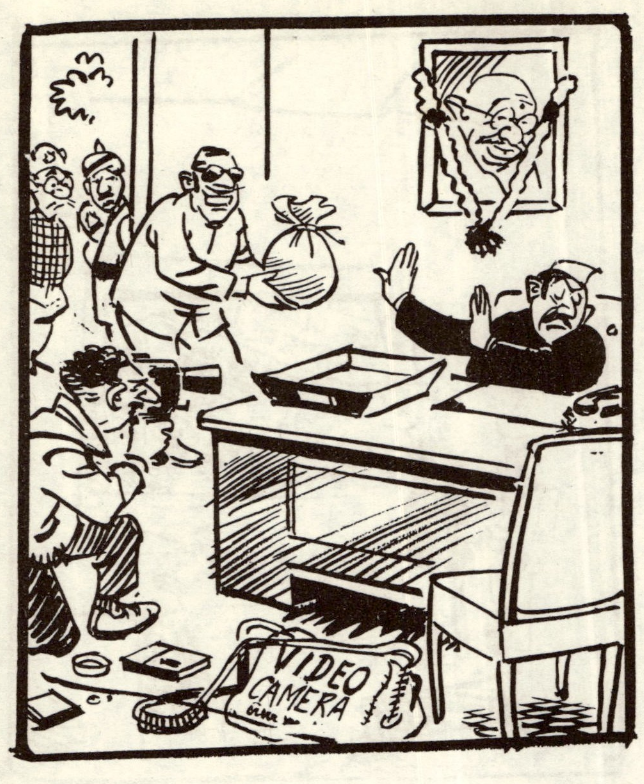

It is for showing at the election meetings how clean he is.

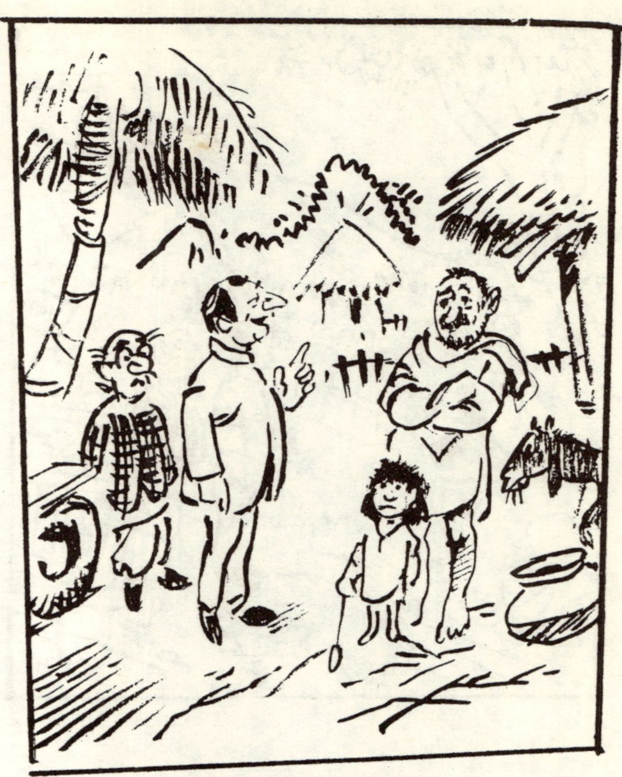

No *water? In the city, we don't have water either. You are lucky you don't have electric power. We have, but it's cut all the time!*

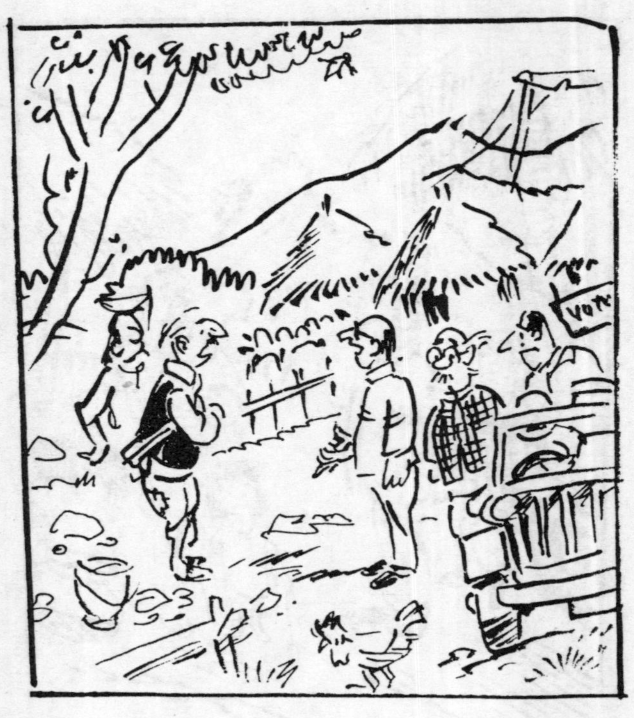

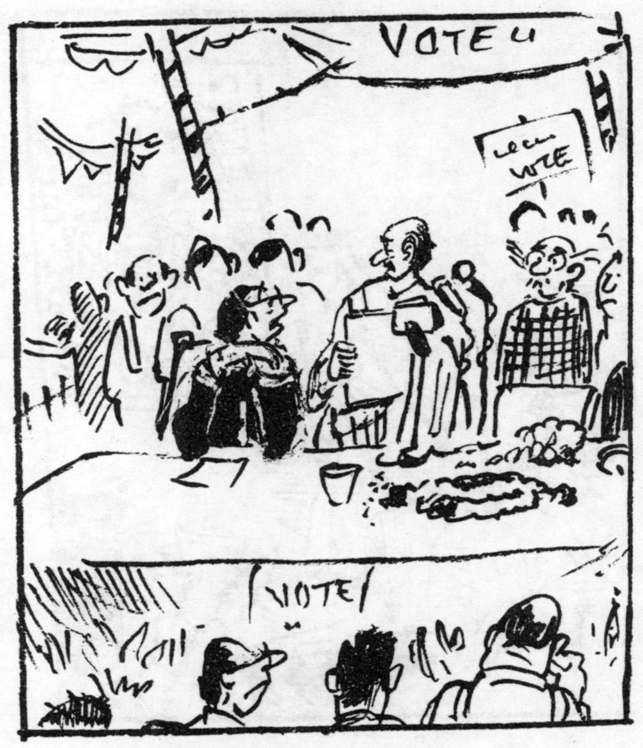

Finished? But you have not yet made any nasty personal attack on their leaders. It is expected in the campaign speeches during this election!

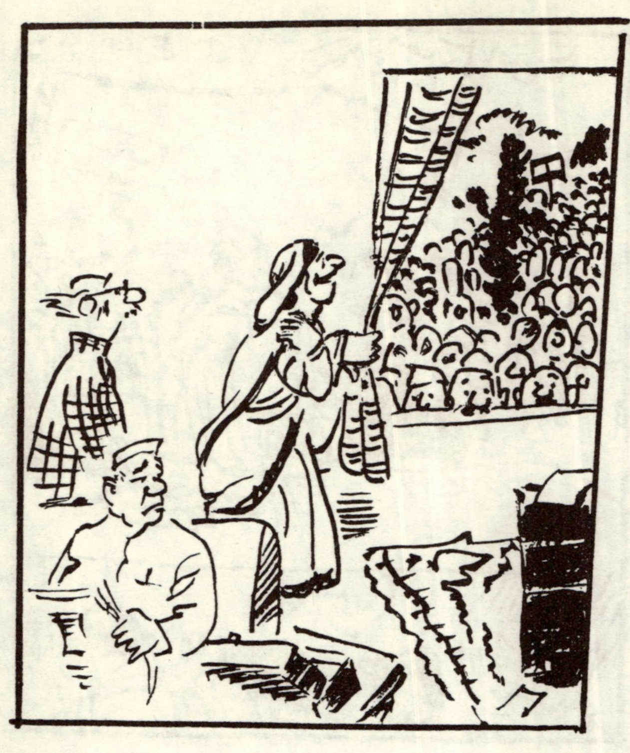

All your supporters! You will have no end of trouble if when the results are out you win and become CM and form a cabinet!

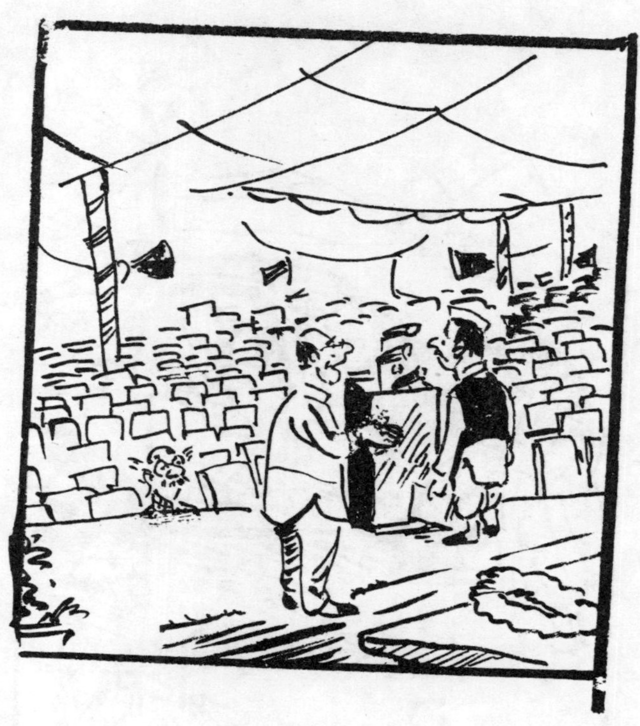

Please go ahead with your address, sir. I bet they are all watching you on TV...

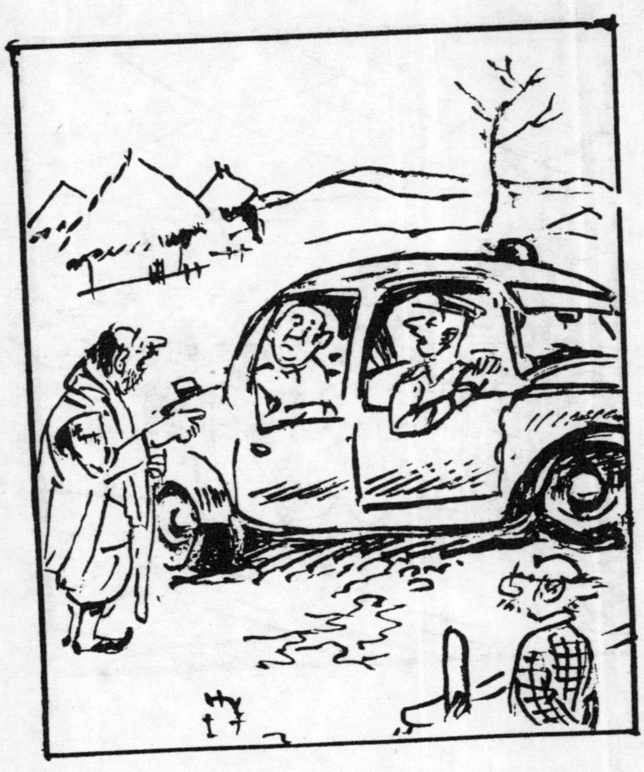

No, *he is not asking for money, sir. He wants that bottle of drinking water you have kept next to you on the seat. This a terribly drought-affected area, sir.*

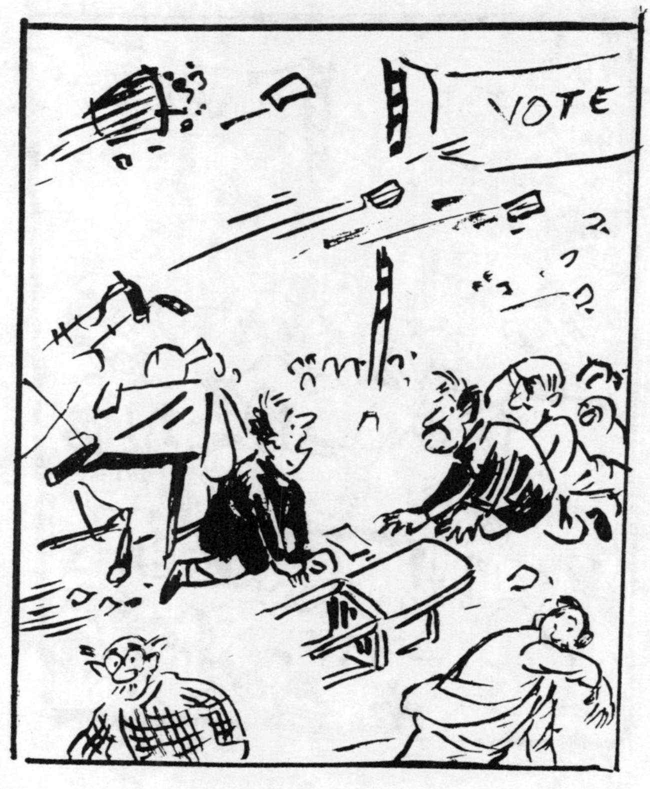

I told that idiot, my speech-writer, to strike off the last sentence in the fifth para of the speech and he didn't. I'm so sorry!

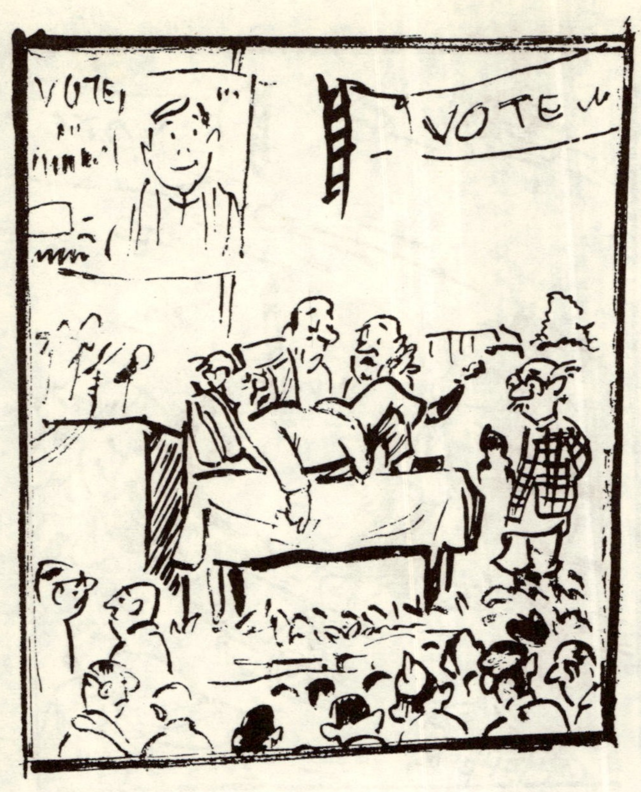

Poor man is completely tired out. Since six in the morning he has been going around addressing meetings!

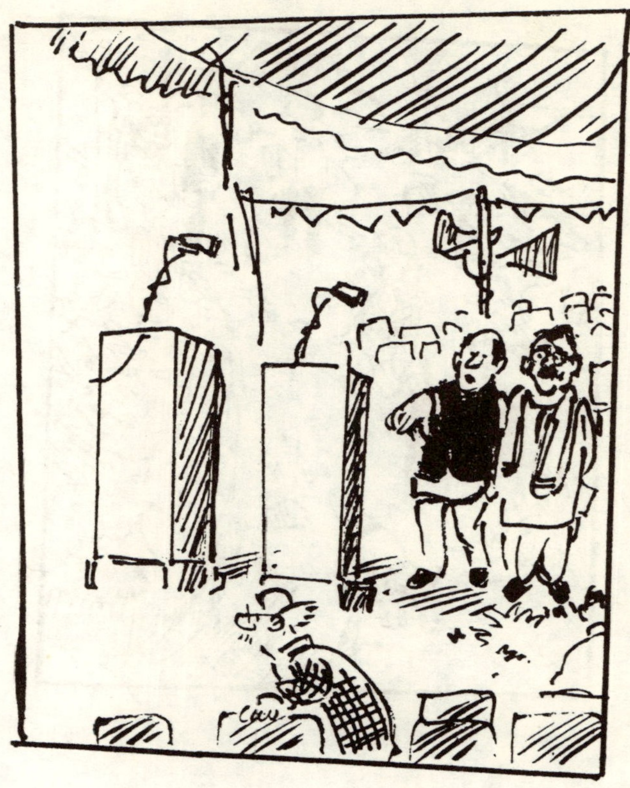

Just as you wanted... That mike is for your speech and this one here is to air your inner voice!

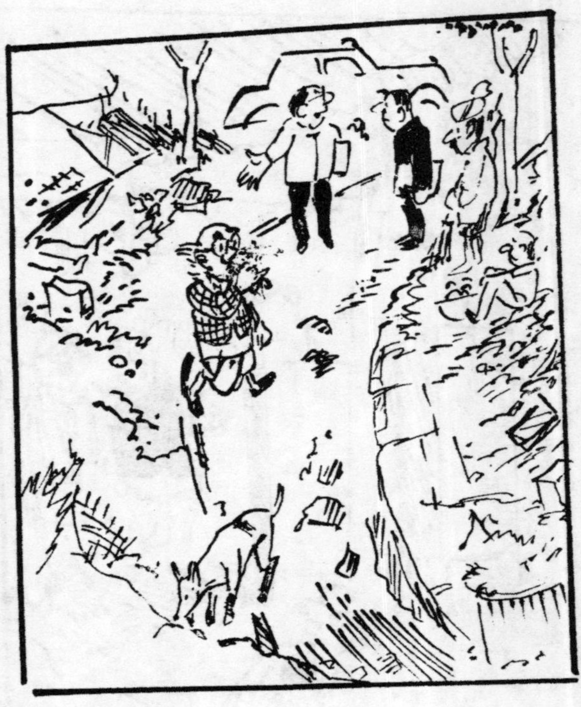

True, the Yatra is passing this way. But don't clean up the place and fill up the potholes. It will be violation of conduct rules—using the tax-payer's money for election purpose!

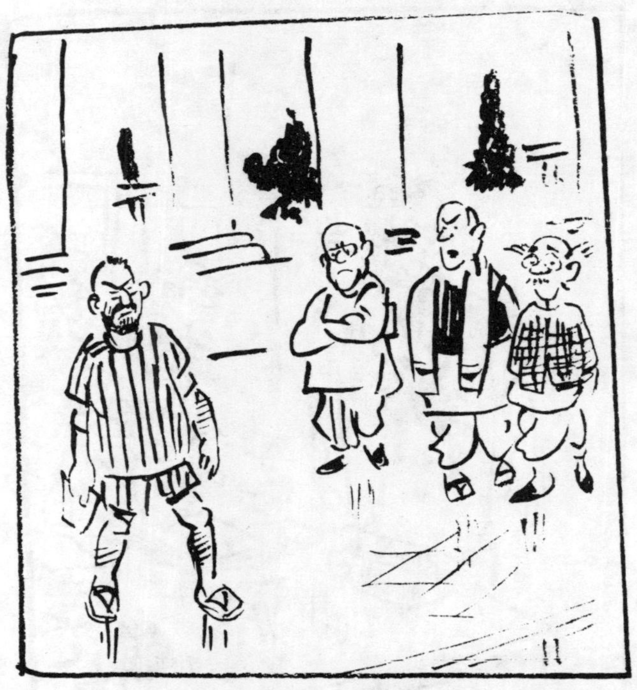

At least these guys should be ordered not to show off that they are tainted so blatantly!

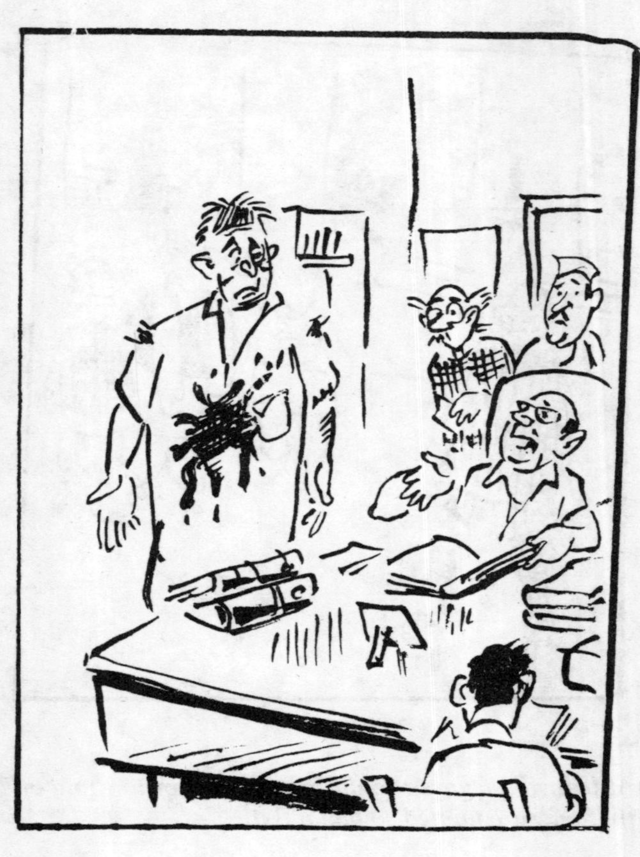

I can't do anything, sir! So sorry, this behaviour of his does not come under the violation of conduct rules!

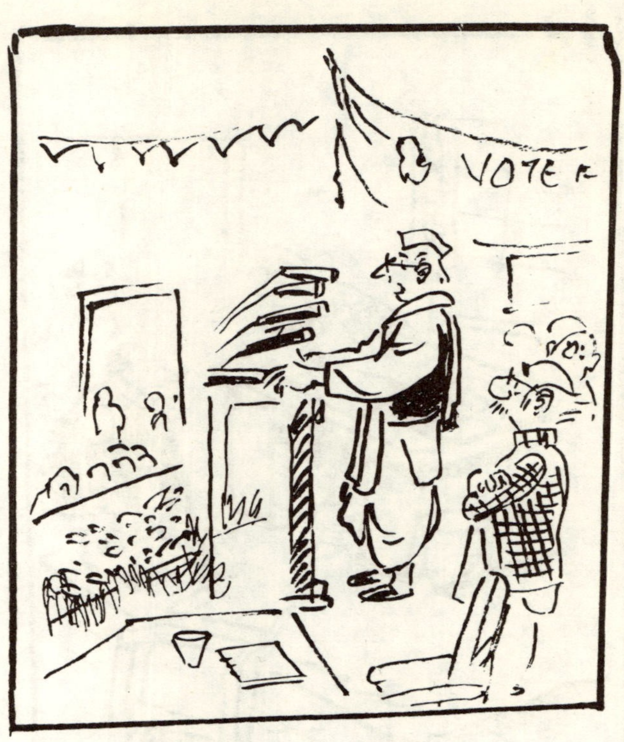

Brothers, cousins, sisters, brothers-in-law, daughters, sons and grandchildren... For our party to win, we must stay united till the polls are over.

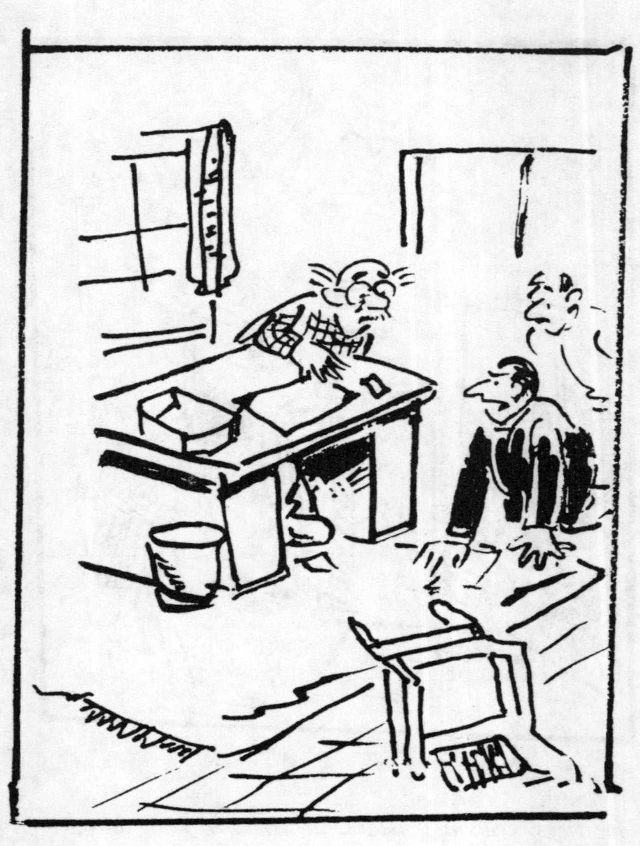

Sulking like this won't do. If you wish to be the CM, first you must get a ticket, a constituency, campaign, and then if you win...

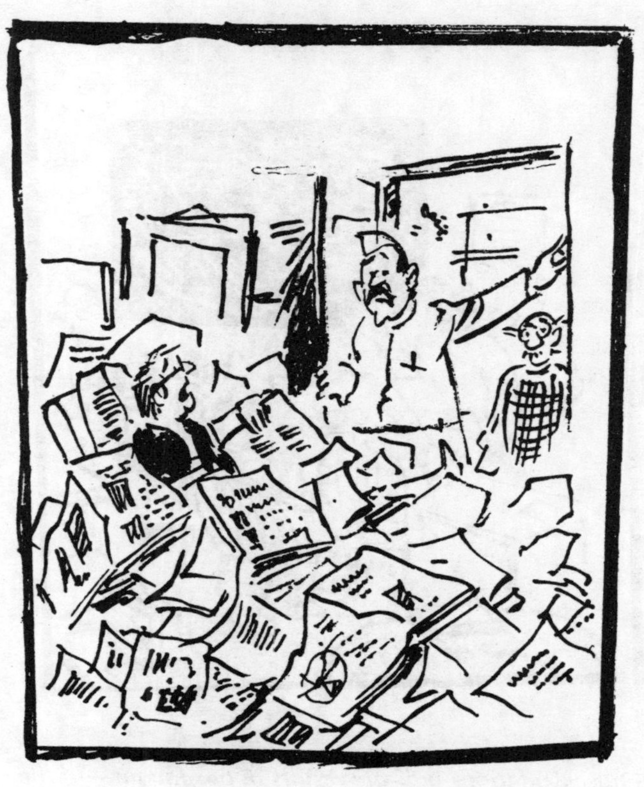

I read all the poll analysis and predictions in detail but can't make out if we are losing or winning!

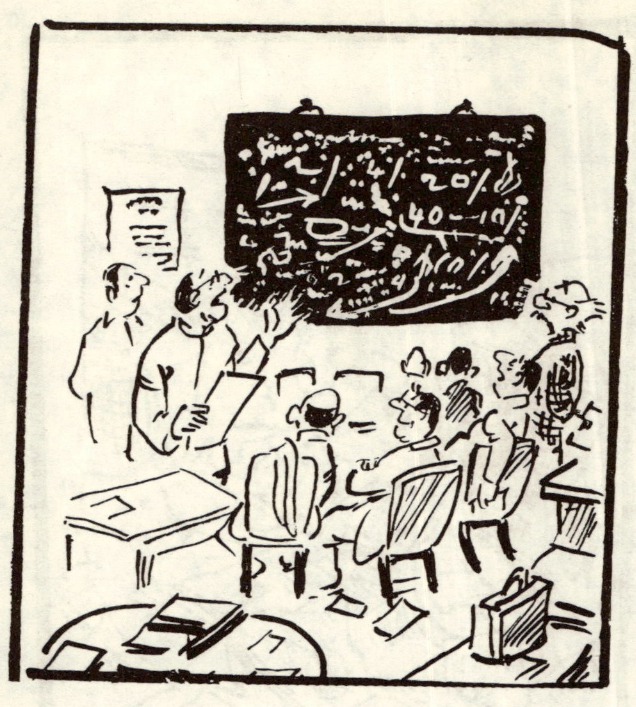

Our calculations indicate results in our favour—of the 40%, 12% will surely vote for us. Of this, 10% may go in favour of the Opposition but 13% are bound to change their mind and support the 18% of the rest of...

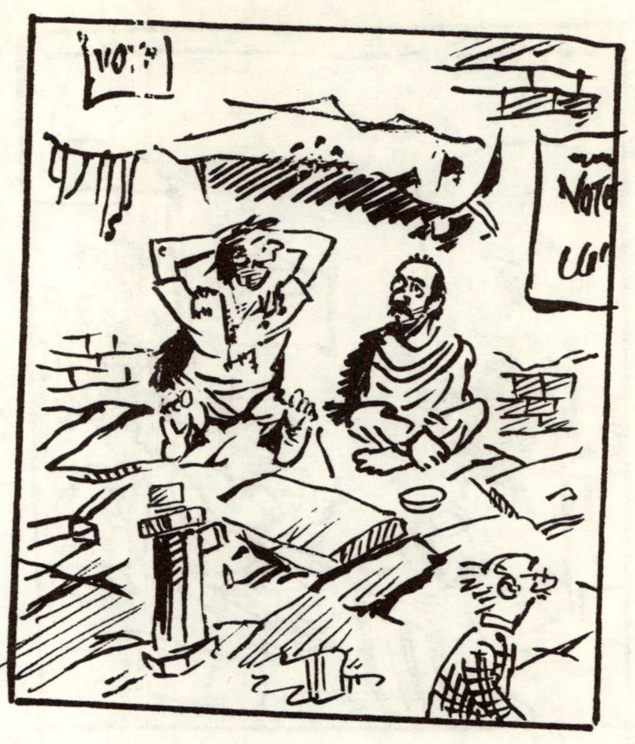

He has promised clean, level pavements for us. I hope he wins!

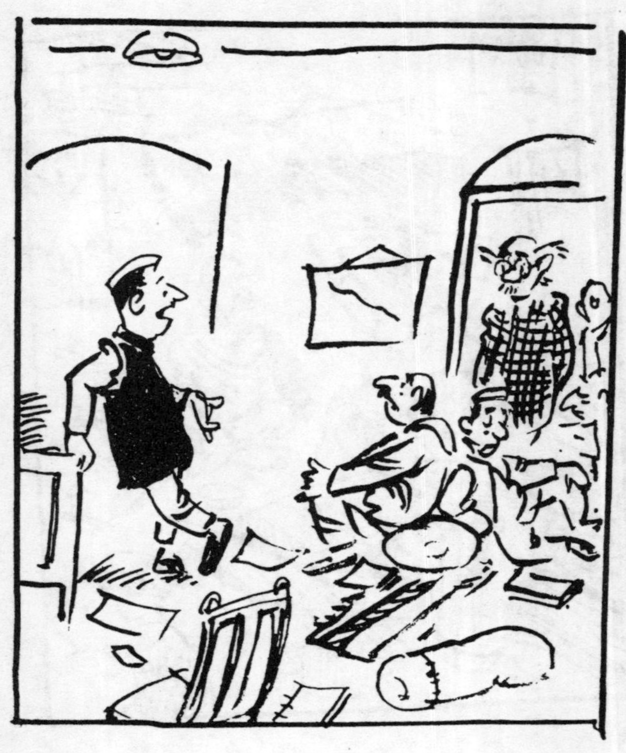

We lost the election. Now we must devote our time to improve the lot of the common man, removing poverty, corruption and so on...

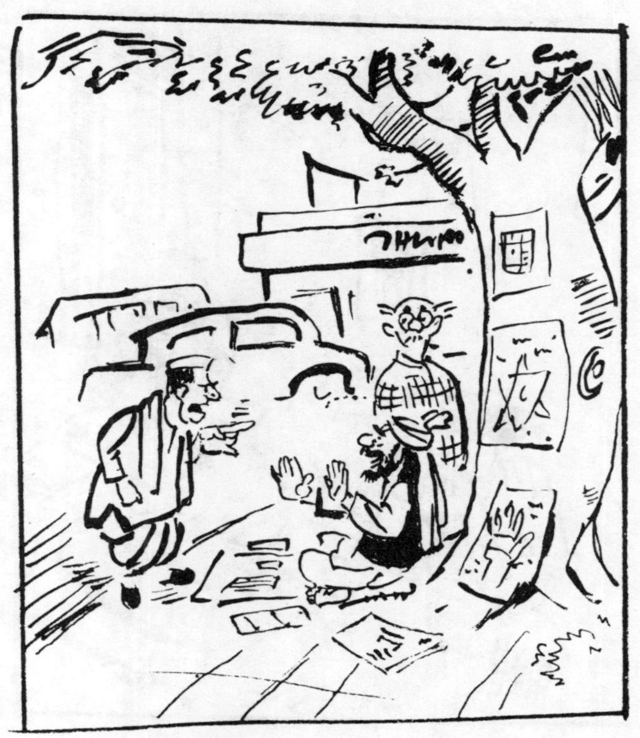

Don't get angry that you lost the election. I predicted you would win based on opinion polls in the newspapers. I knew you would lose on the basis of my astrological study, but didn't tell you that to keep you happy.

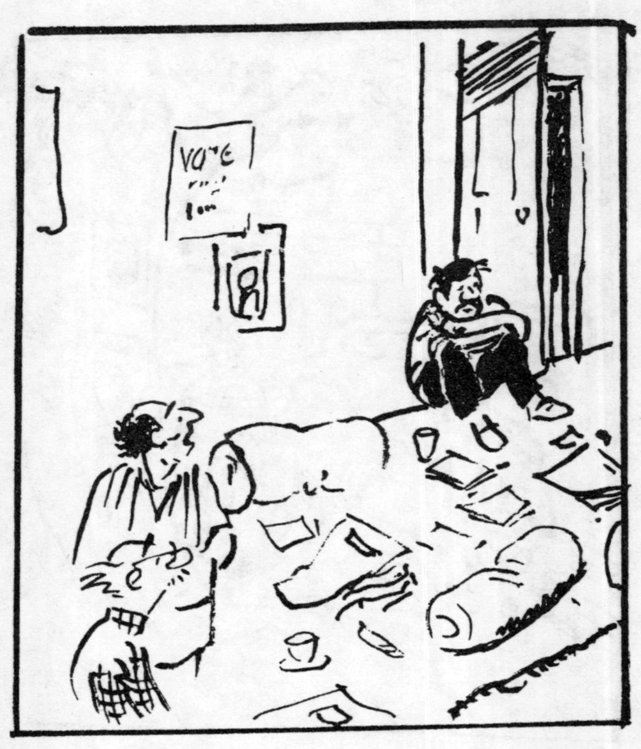

He lost because people did not vote for him. That's OK, he says. But to lose in spite of booth capturing, bribing and intimidation makes him feel miserable!

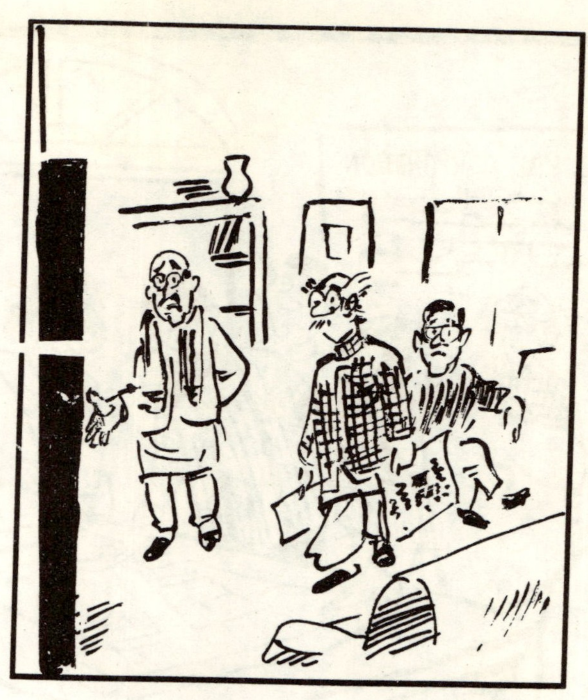

What have you done to yourself? Are you on protest? Wearing a fool's cap, painting your nose red, wearing rags! Don't you read newspapers? Sonia has decided not to be the PM!

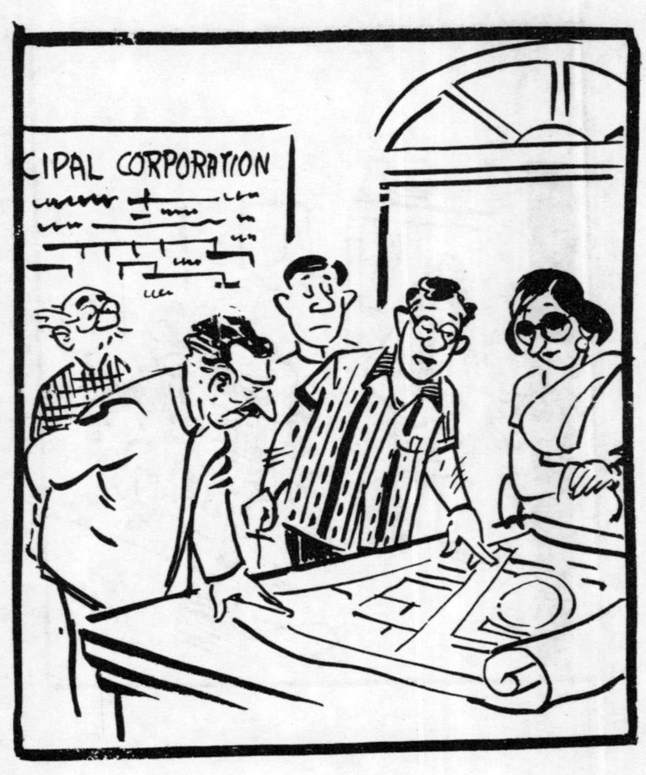

We have plans of beautifying this road from here to
here, sir, by removing the garbage.

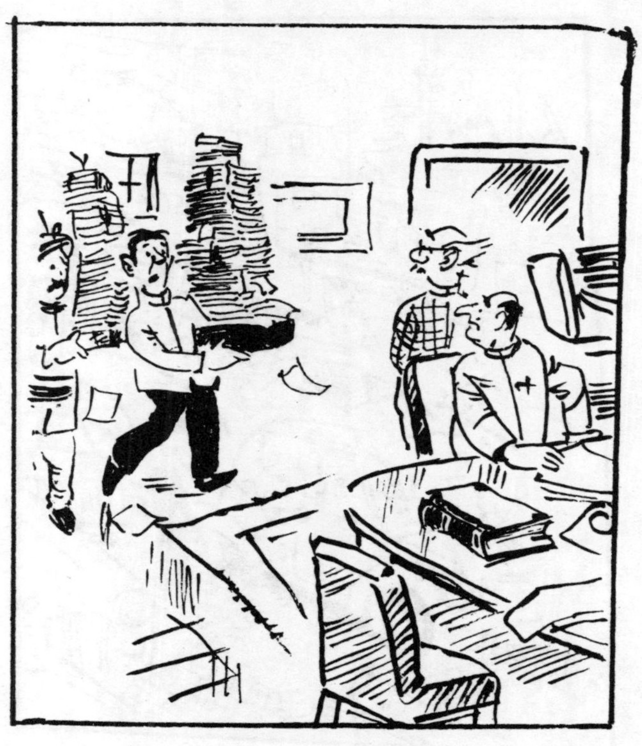

Here are the clarifications you sought for some of the
statements the officer made during his interrogation,
sir!

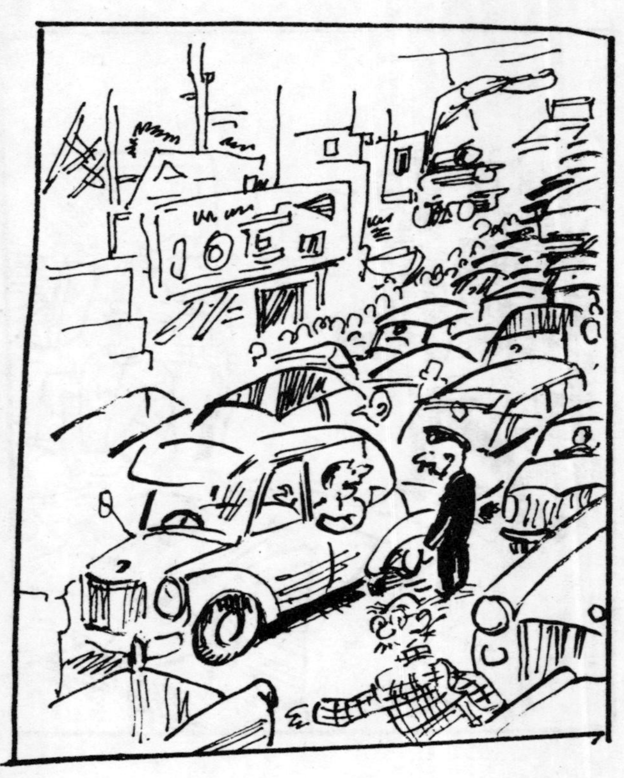

The car driver? The traffic takes such a long time to move, the driver got tired and asked if he could go and have a cup of tea and return. I said OK.

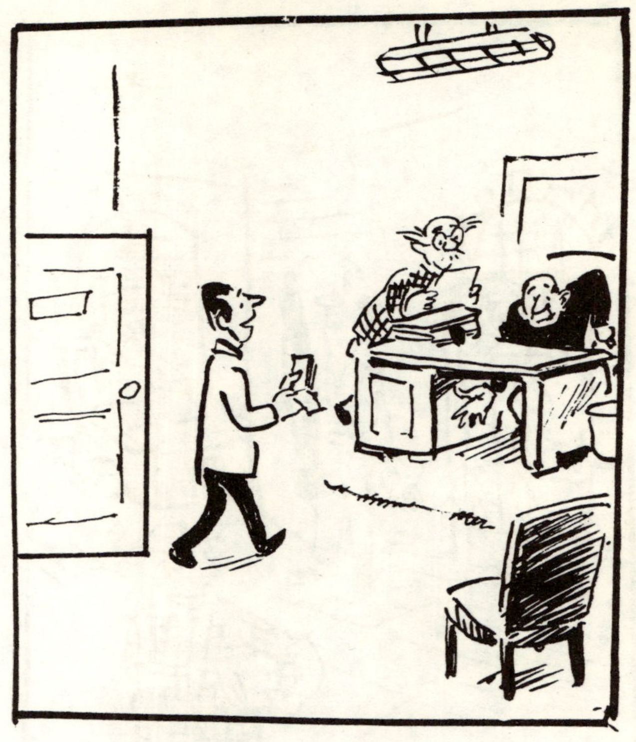

No *need* to receive it like *that, sir. It's your own money.
You had sent me to the bank to encash your cheque, sir!*

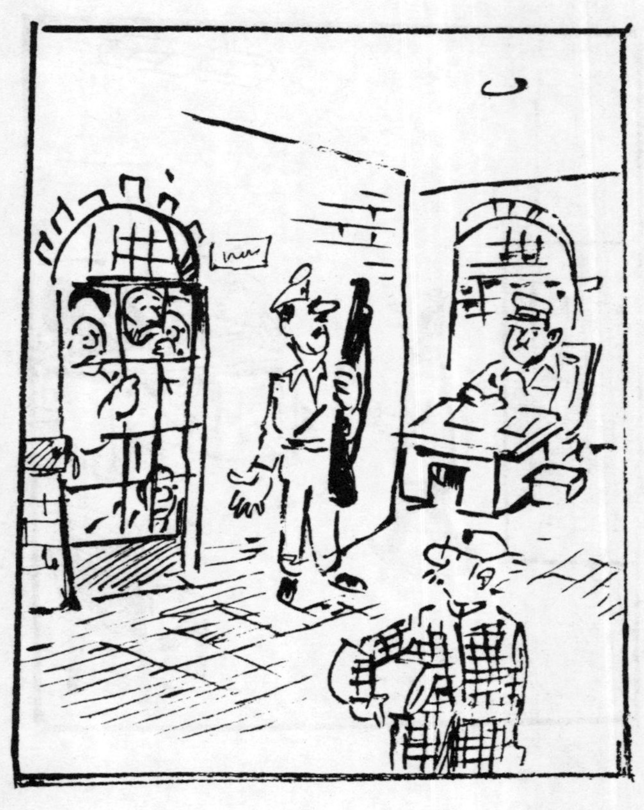

Better install a TV in their cells, sir. They go on pestering me for the latest cricket score all the time!

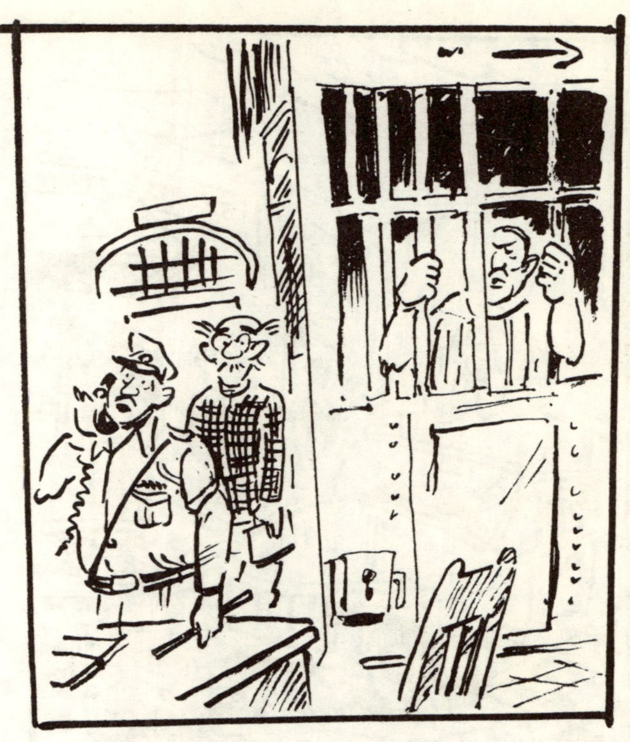

He is threatening to go on revealing more and more names of ministers, police officers and officials, as long as he is kept in custody, sir.

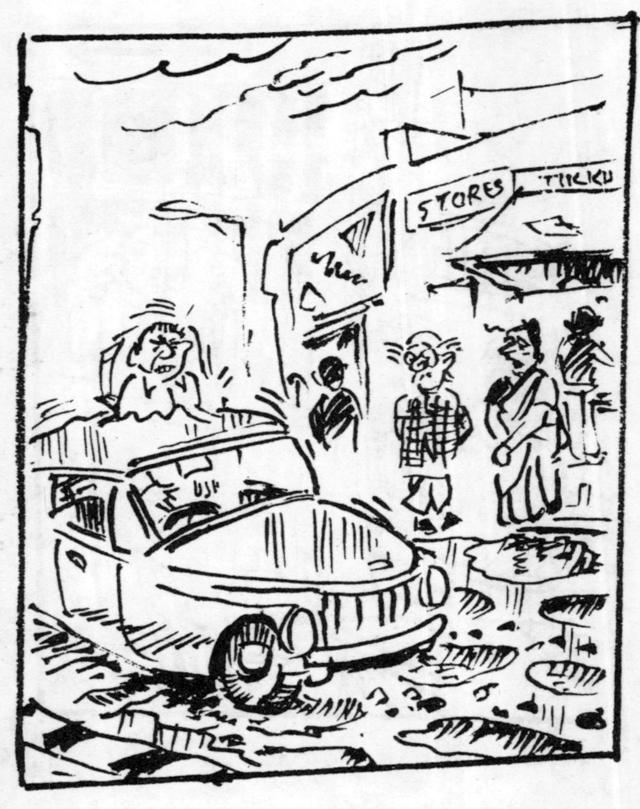

Look, *what the bumpy, pothole-ridden road has done to that poor driver!*

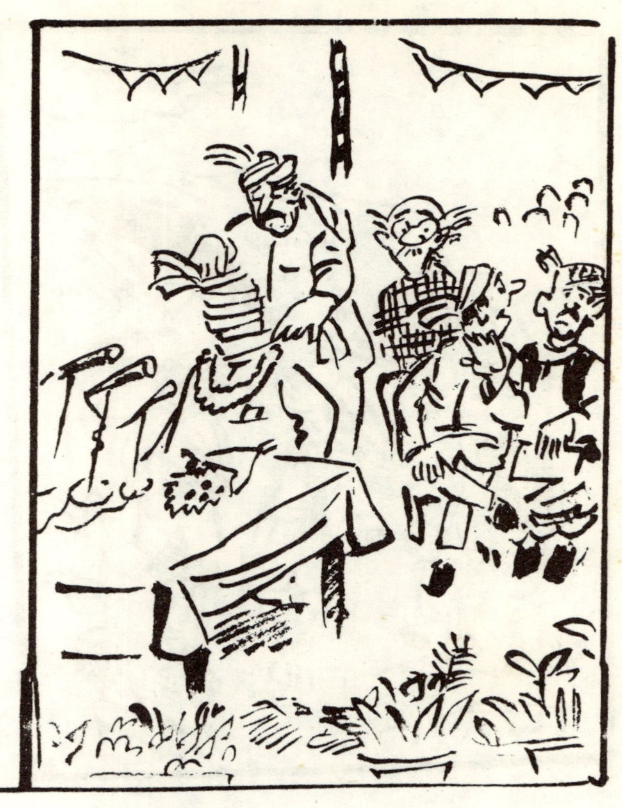

*Someone who knows how to tie the turban should have
been asked to attend to our chief guest's turban!*

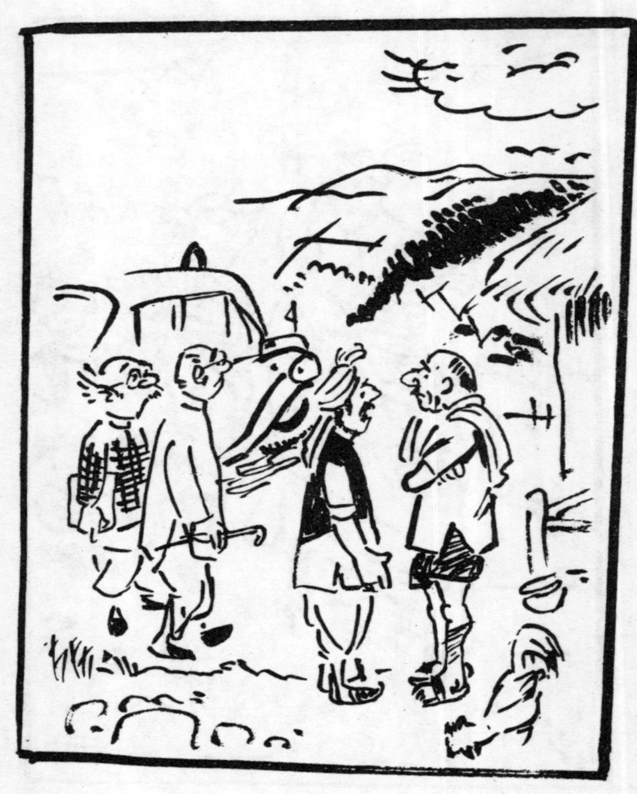

It's no use complaining to him about our difficulties. Elections are over, you see. He has come to visit his farmhouse.

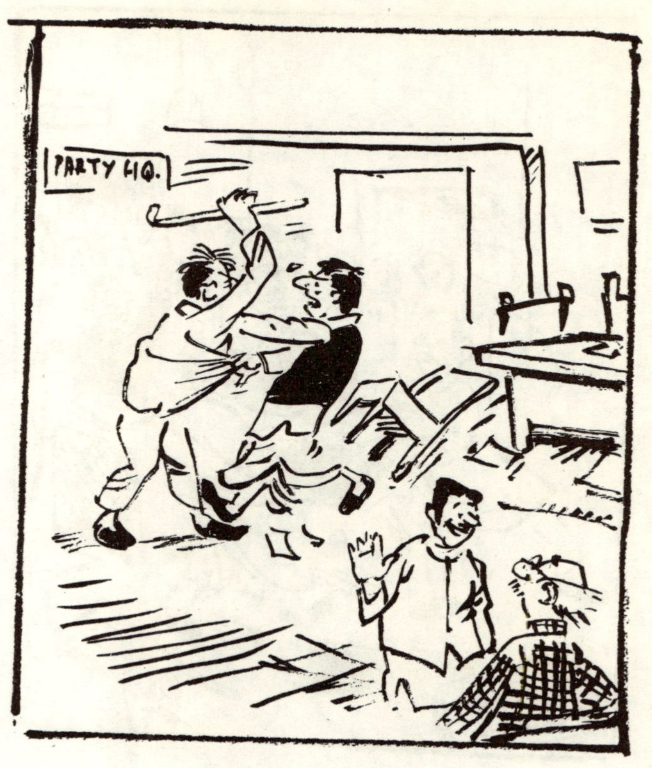

*They say it has nothing to do with politics. Then it must
be something to do with cricket!*

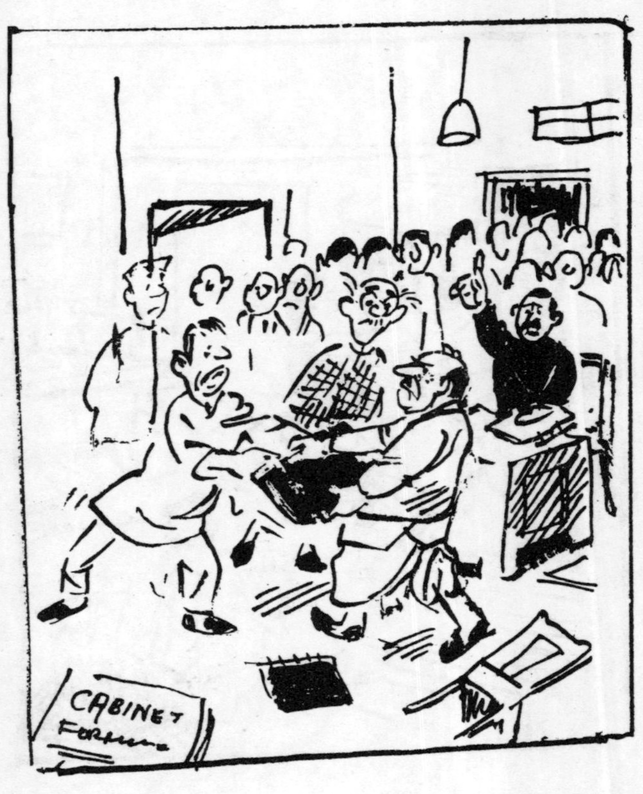

Friends, just a minute! This is no way to get the portfolio you wish to have. I'll have to decide it, please!

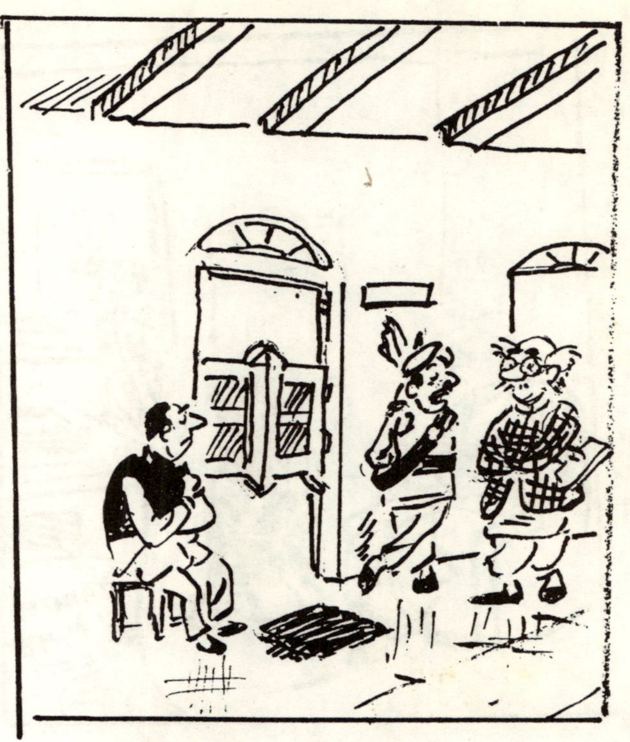

There aren't enough rooms to accommodate the new
ministers. That one happens to be a minister without
portfolio. We could seat him there.

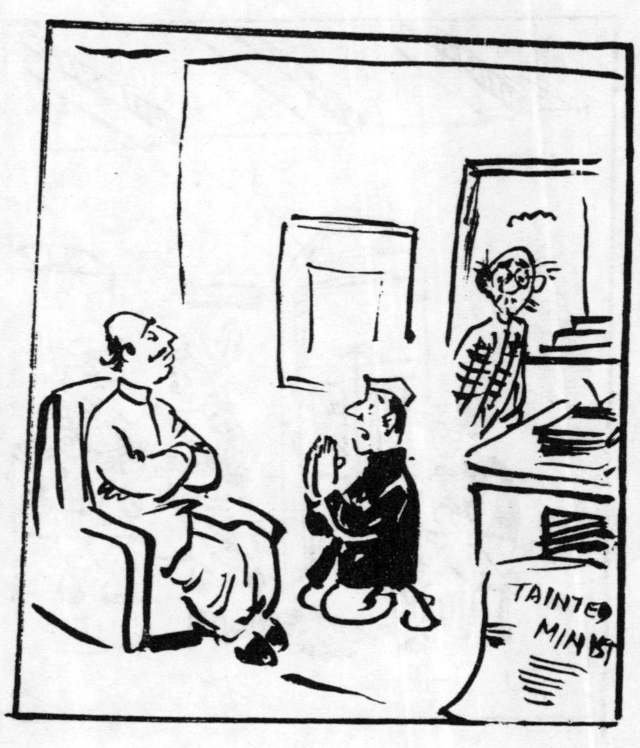

Please put in your resignation voluntarily to protect the name of our party and my government! Please.

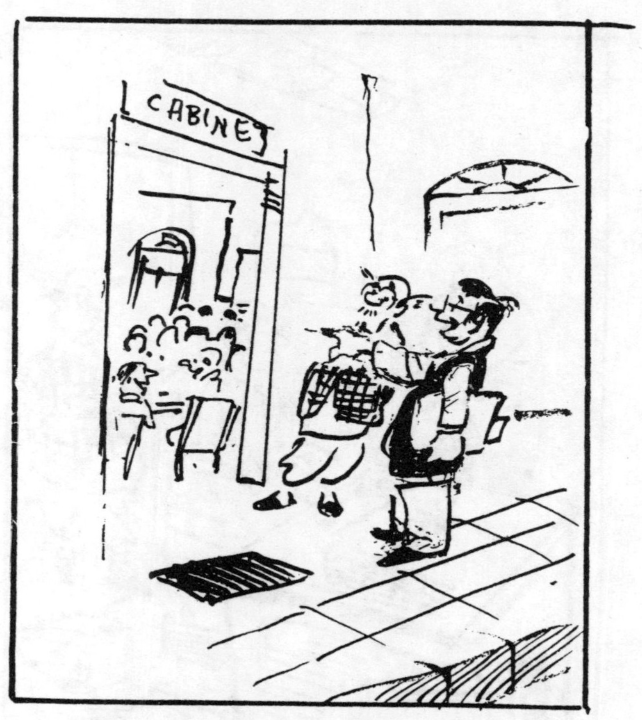

We work as one big family here. That's my son, next is my brother, that one is my son-in-law, then my sister's father-in-law...

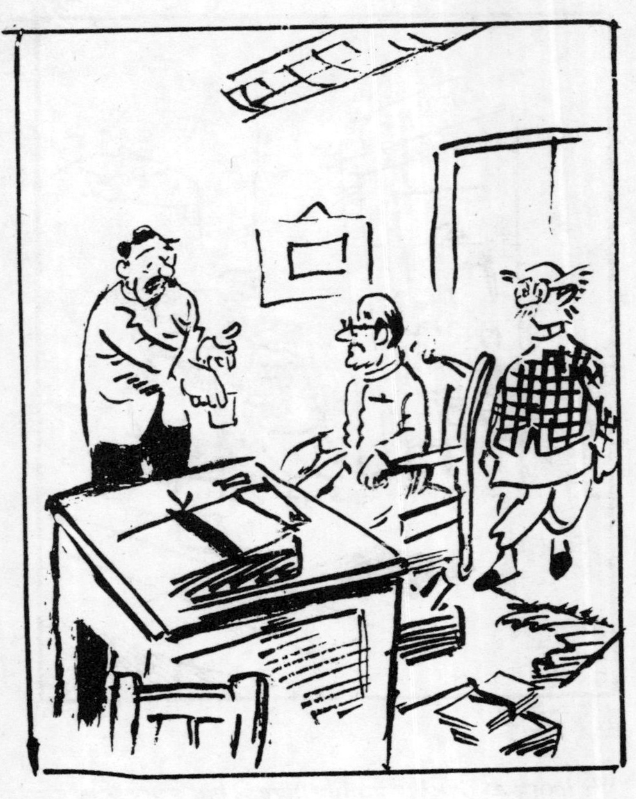

I have drafted the common minimum programme, sir. I reduced it to the maximum I could—not any further. Sorry, sir.

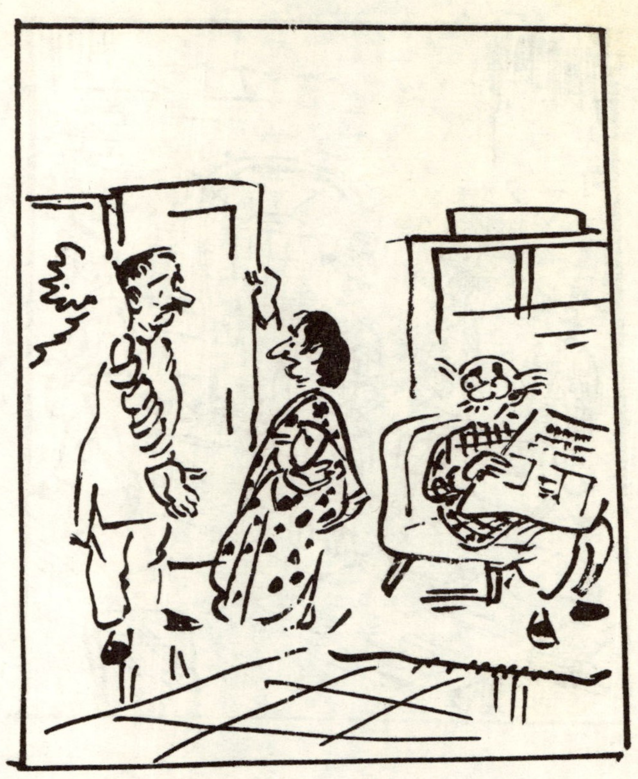

*Again you have let your alliance partner twist your arm!
You had better resign from politics!*

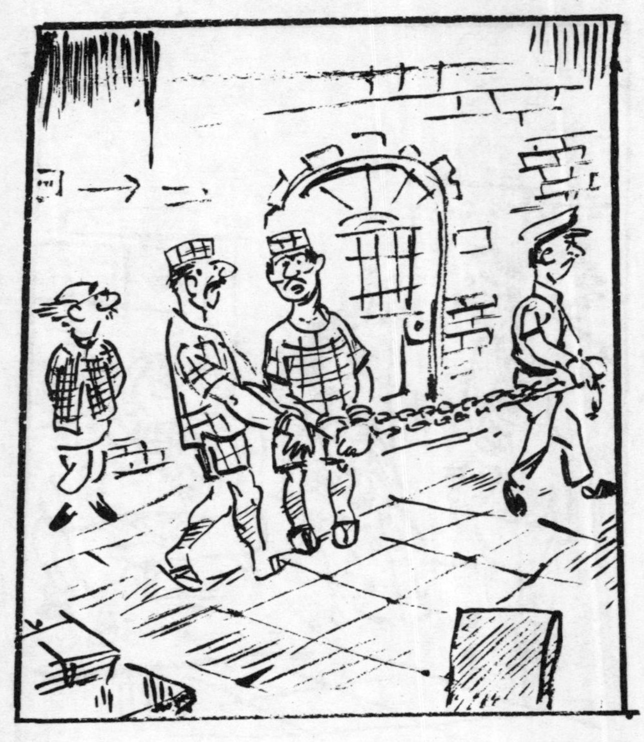

What am I going to do after my release? Join some political party and fight an election...

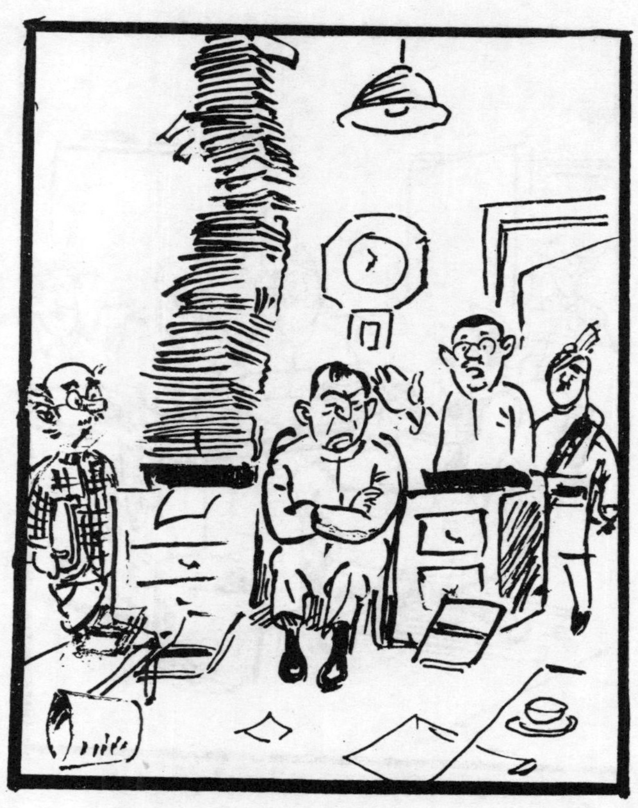

We all know, sir, you don't like the portfolio allotted to you. But, sir, having accepted it you must at least put the files in the 'out' tray.

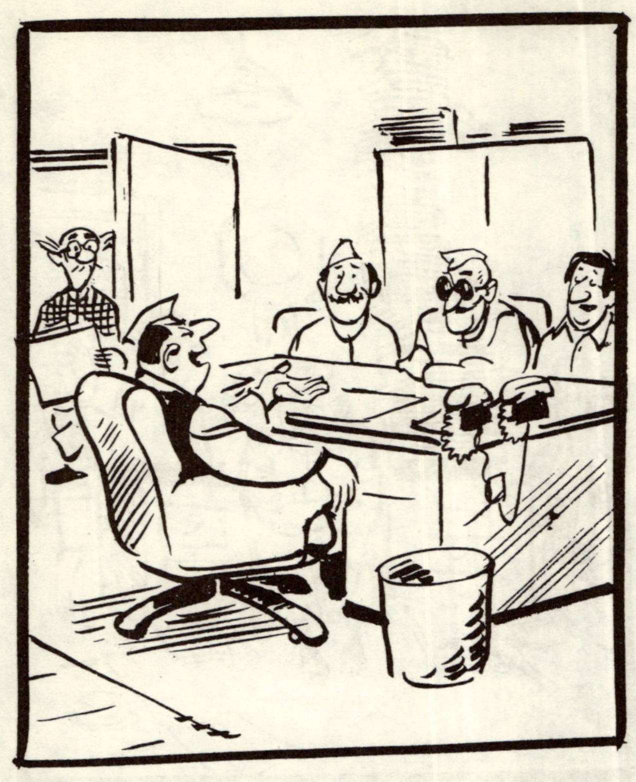

Party's image is damaged, yes! But that's nothing to be alarmed about; it has been damaged many times before!

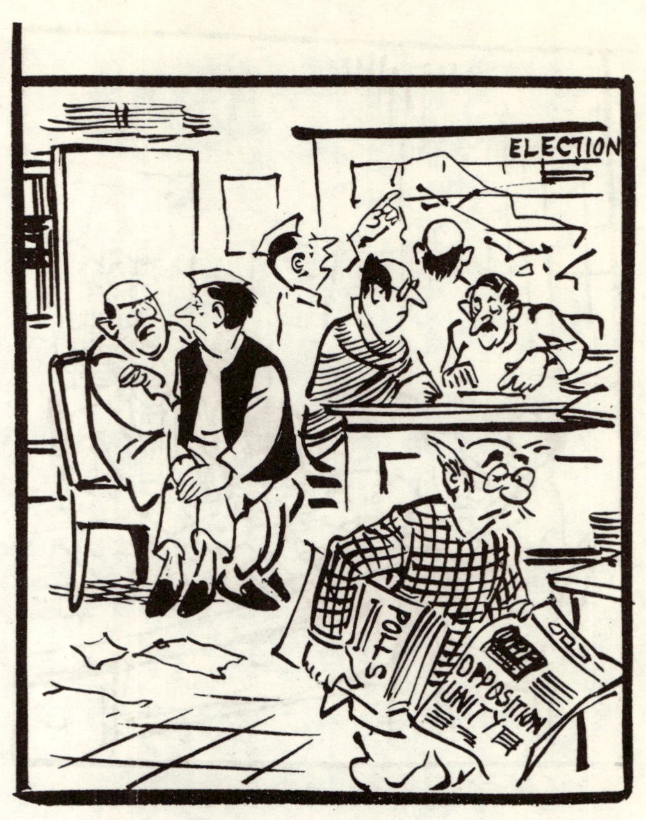

Please, I don't want to spoil the understanding reached between our parties, but 'seat-sharing' or 'seat adjustment' certainly doesn't mean this!

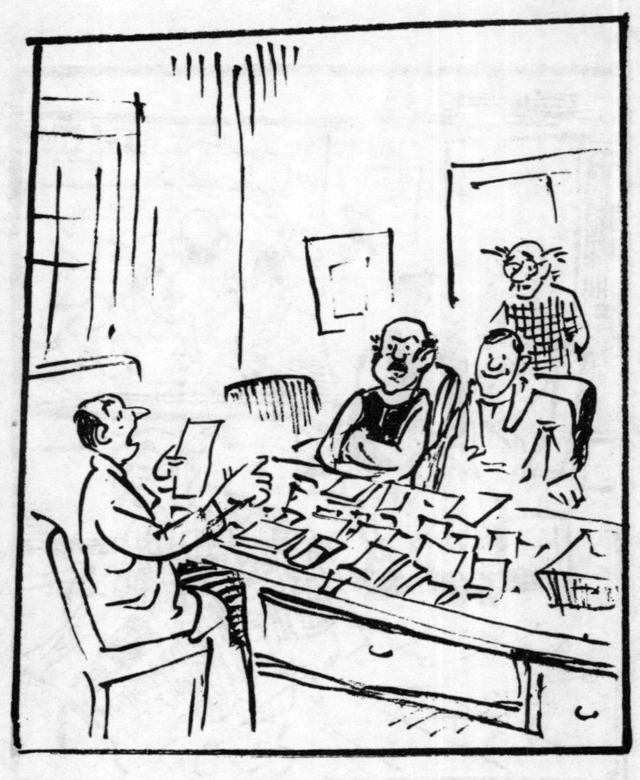

Well, if you don't like that one, here is yet another proposal: you be the CM on Monday, Wednesday and Friday and he will be the CM on the rest of the days. OK?

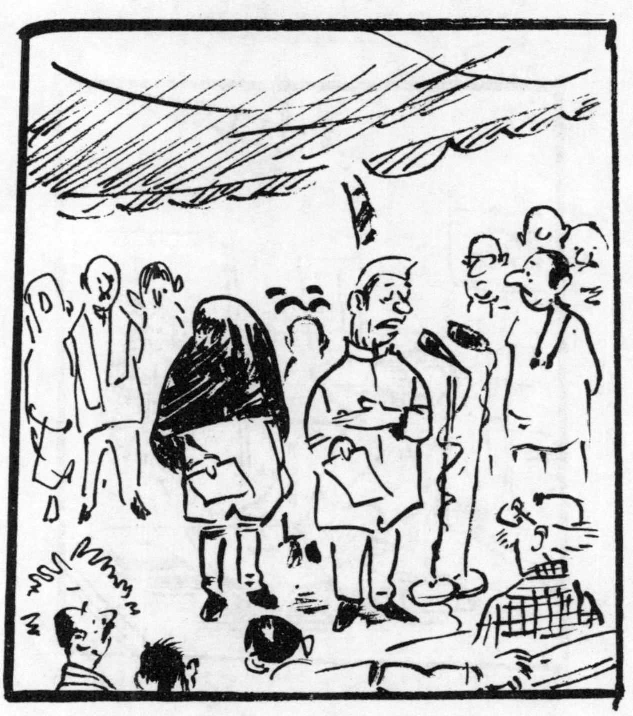

One of our party members wants to make a speech criticizing the leadership on condition of anonymity...

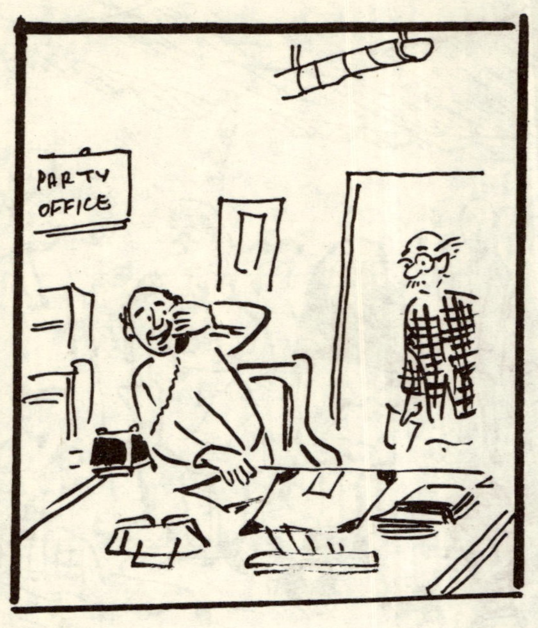

Sorry, I can't come. We have our party infighting session during that time.

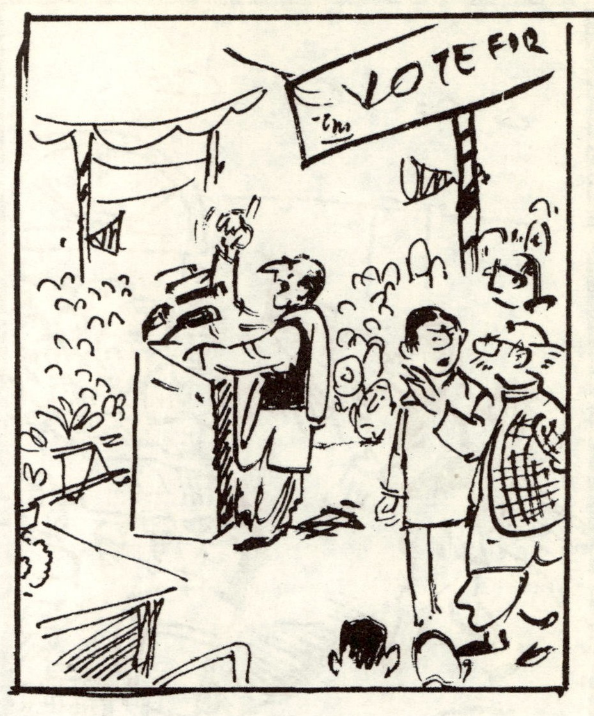

He is criticizing and attacking the government forgetting it is his and he is heading it!

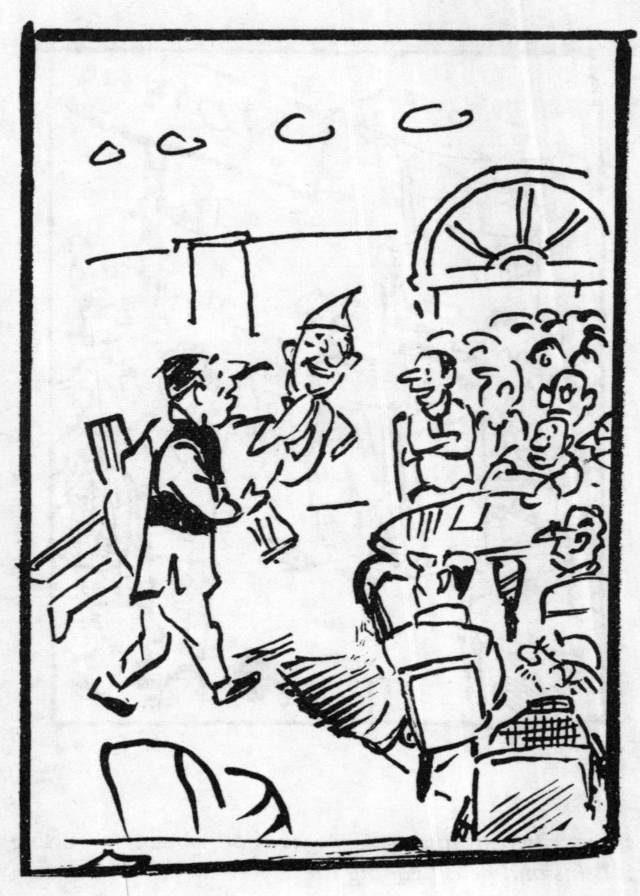

He apologizes for not being able to attend the meeting.
But he has sent his cut-out which he used during the
elections.

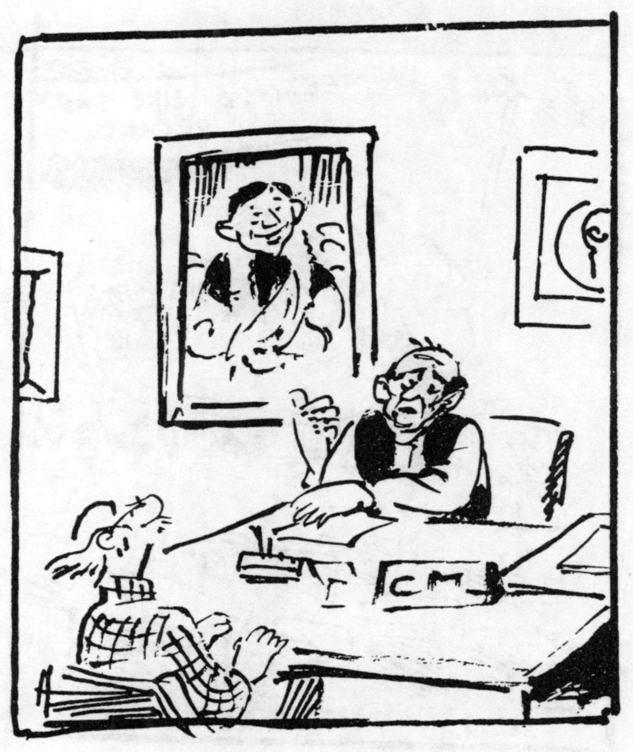

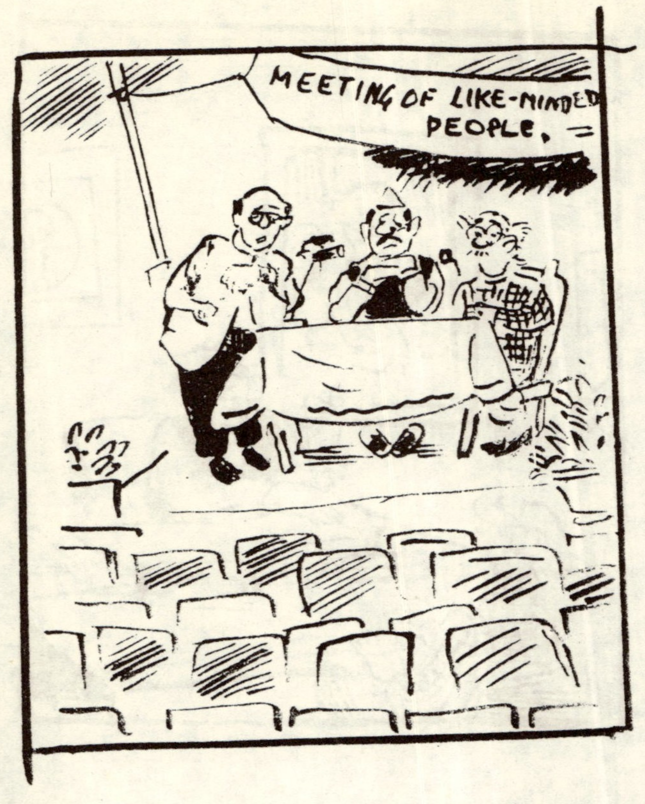

We have waited two hours and not a single like-minded person has turned up, sir. It's no use waiting any more.

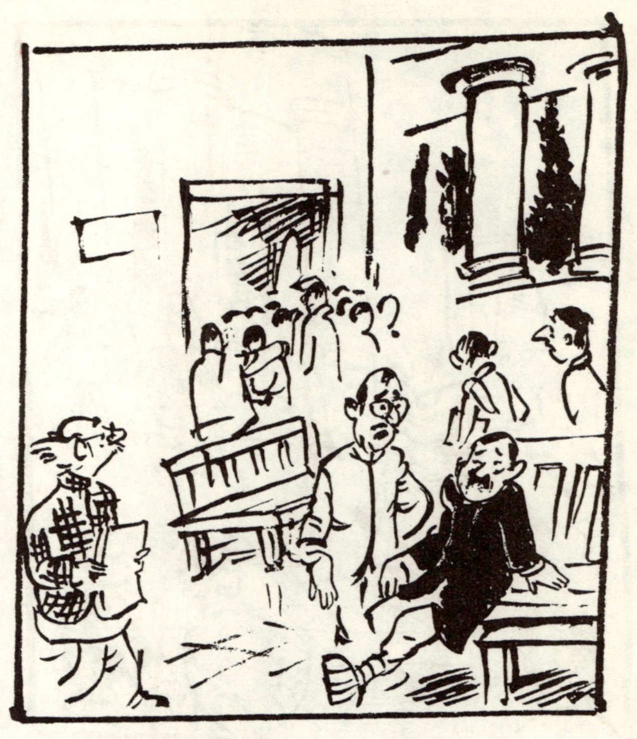

Sprained your ankle, have you? Today there is going to
be a debate on important national issues. How are you
going to participate in the walkouts?

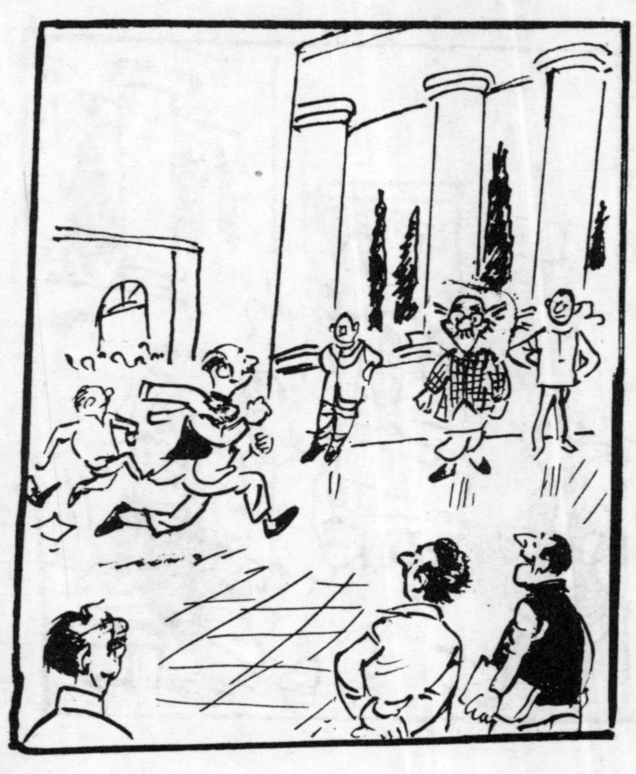

This is a good idea. His party protests in a different way this session. Instead of a walkout, it stages a run-out!

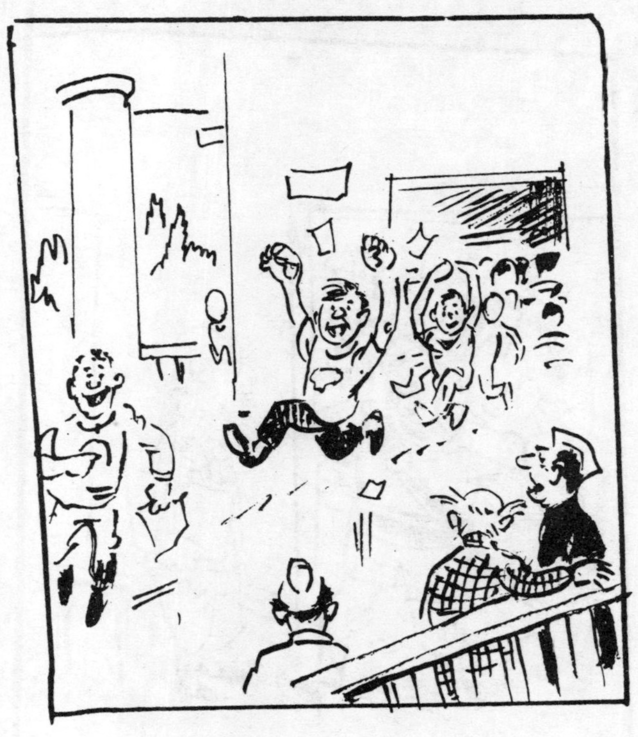

The young MPs *must* be asked to stage the walkouts
with a little more decorum and decency!

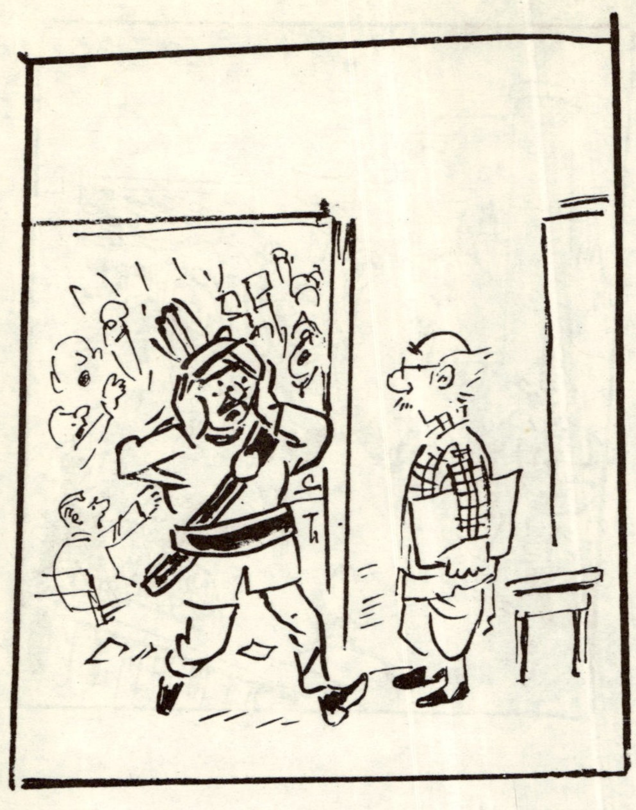

Whether they are staging a walkout or not, I am! I can't stand any more the din they create... shouting and thumping the desks and so on!

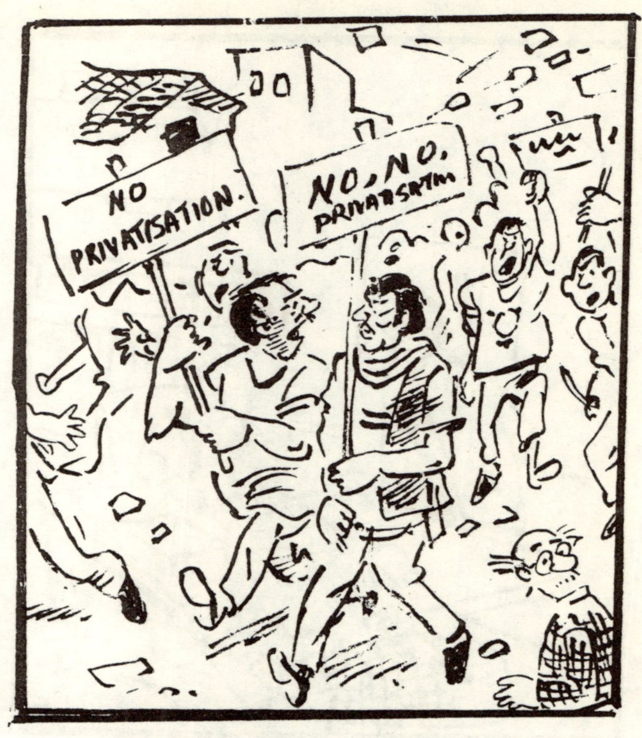

By the way, what is 'privatisation'?

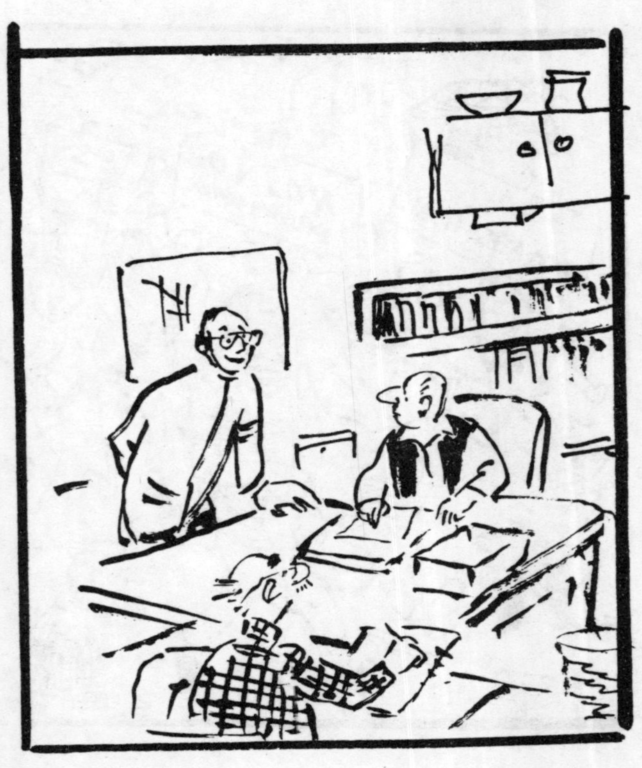

No, don't hike the price by 10% all at once. People will resent it and protest! Hike it by 20% first and after a week cut it to 10%. People will appreciate your concern for them!

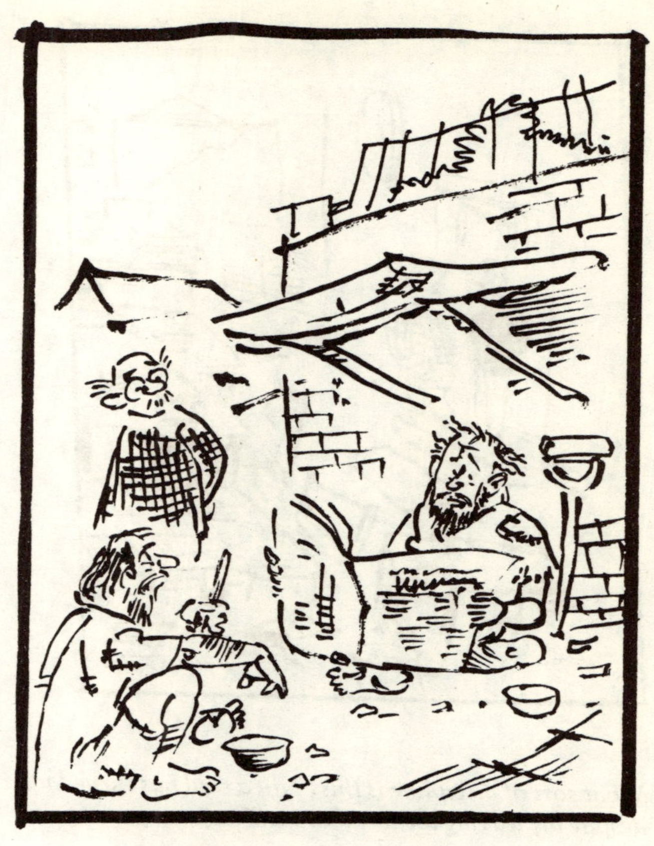

Prices of petrol, diesel, gas have been hiked! How do they expect people with money to survive? Poor things!

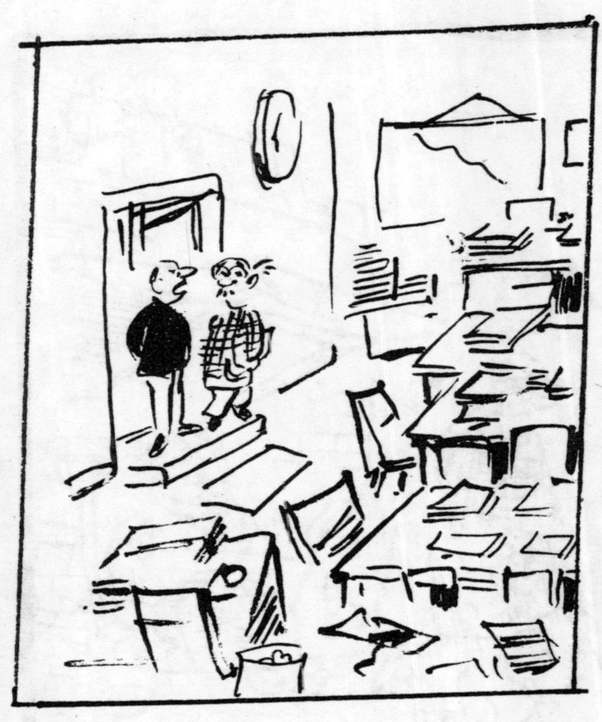

What sort of discipline is this? Not a soul has turned up despite my leaking the fact that I will be paying a surprise visit!

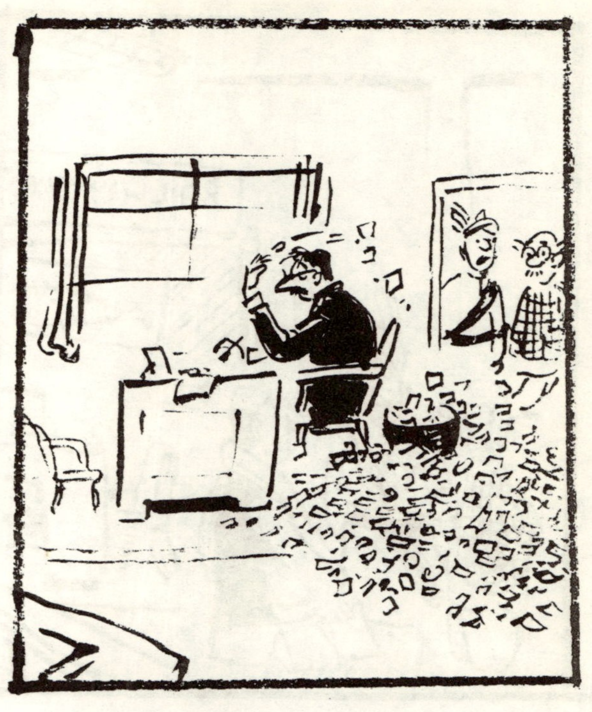

He wants to resign voluntarily. He has been trying to draft the resignation letter since the morning!

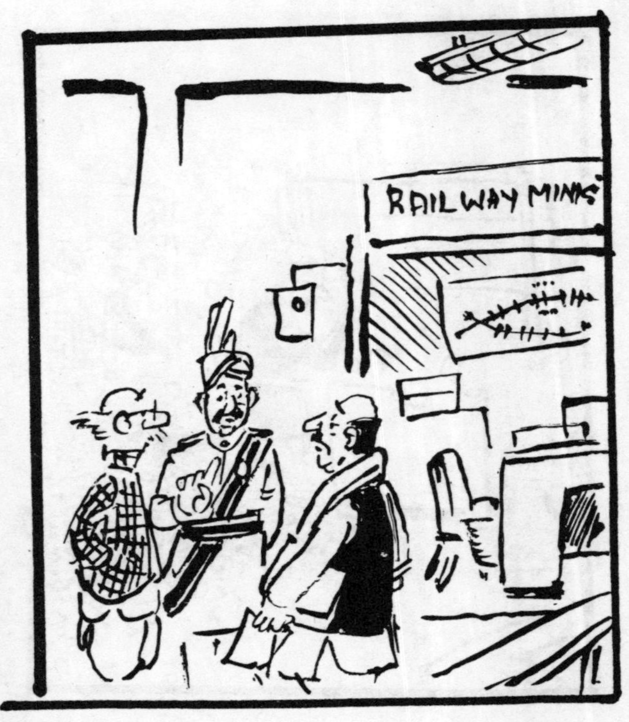

No, *no, you can't say he has not done anything to avert rail accidents. He has sacked and transferred several senior officials, engineers and others connected with the railways.*

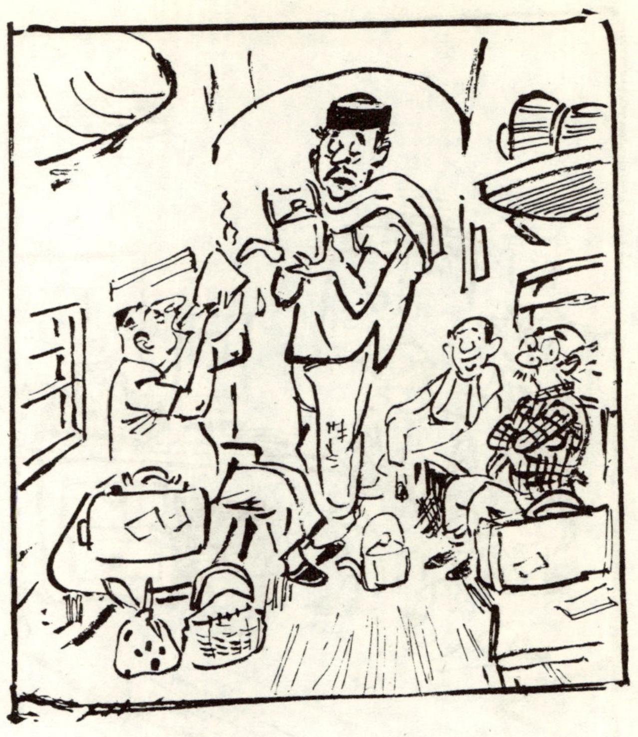

The present rail ministry withdrew teacups and replaced them with mud cups; now it has withdrawn that also and the tea is served in this manner!

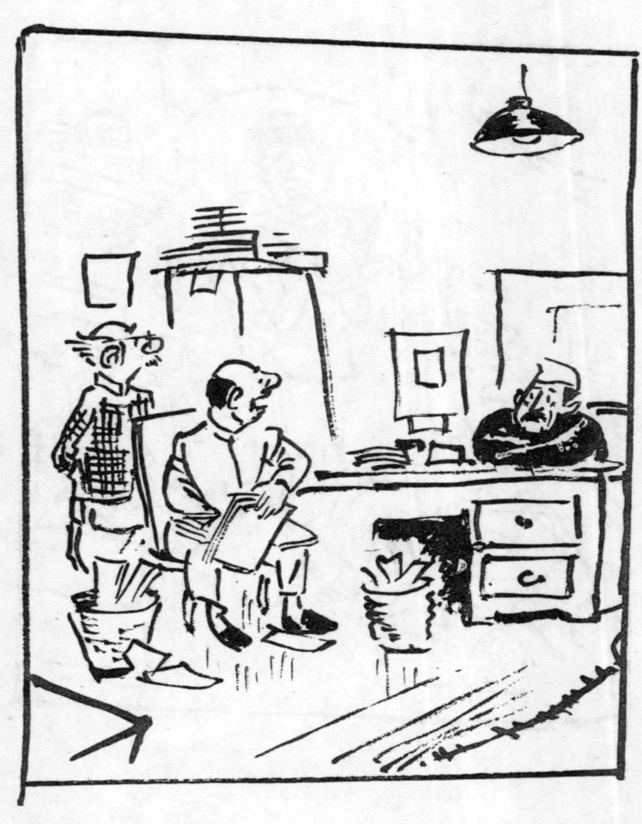

Shall I discard these election speeches promising water, food, electricity, sir? Or keep them for future elections?

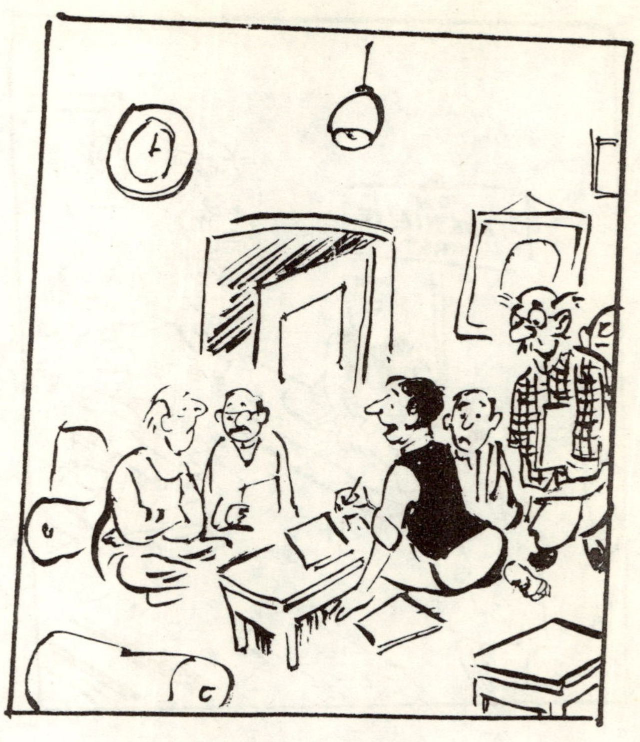

We won the parliamentary polls promising poverty eradication, employment etc. Why not make the same promises for the assembly elections also, sir?

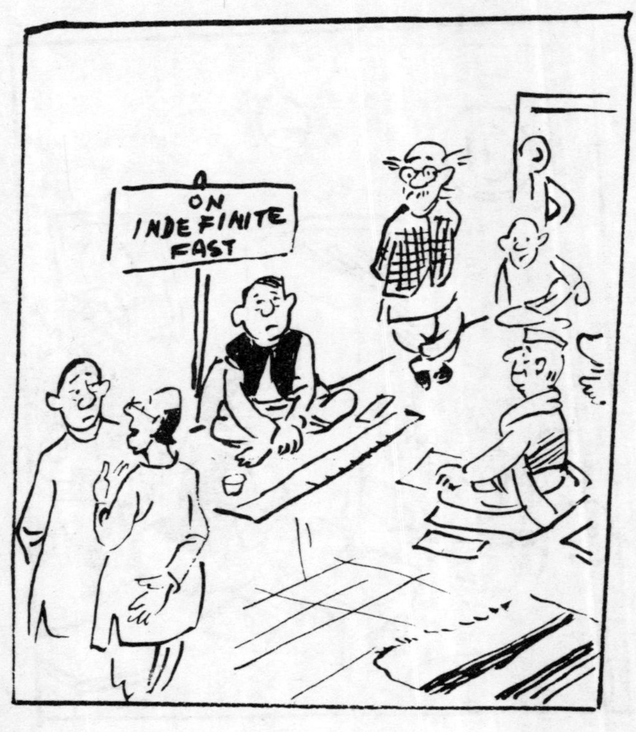

He has agreed to undertake the fast for the sake of our noble cause on the condition he gets a small snack in the morning, a little something like fruits, bread in the afternoon and some biscuits and milk at night, sir. Sounds reasonable.

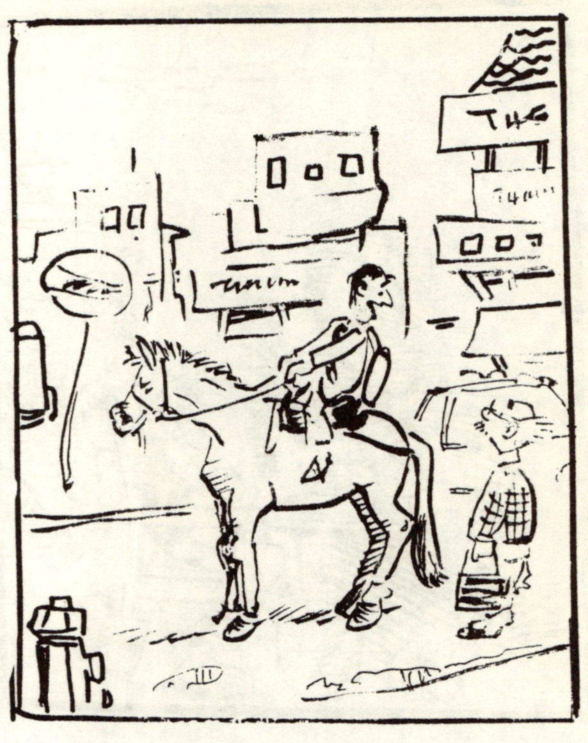

With the motor fuel prices going up every other day, I find this more economical to move around.

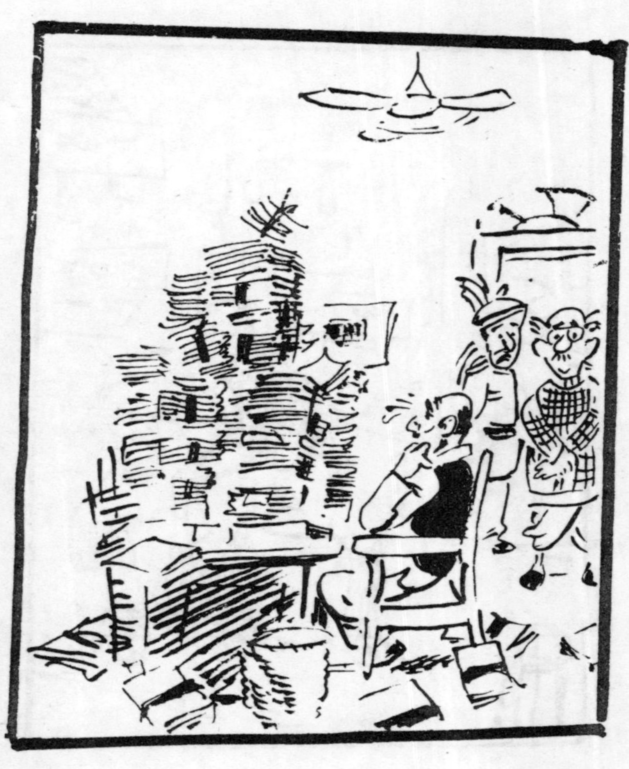

He had not looked at a single file for months thinking he was going to retire soon. Now that he has got an extension, he is worried he has to study all those files and take action!

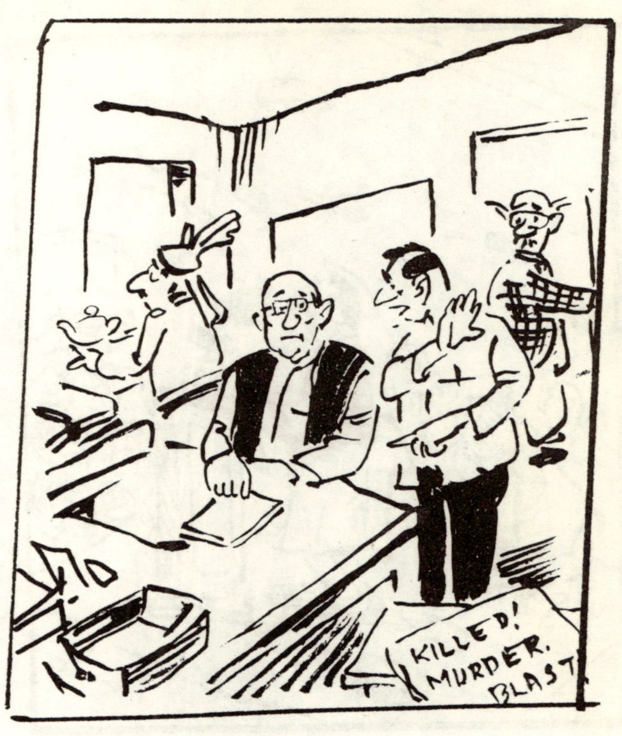

You have declared that you will not tolerate terrorism only six times the whole of last week. They may think you have begun to tolerate them. So, I have added that you will not tolerate terrorism in every para of your speech today, sir!

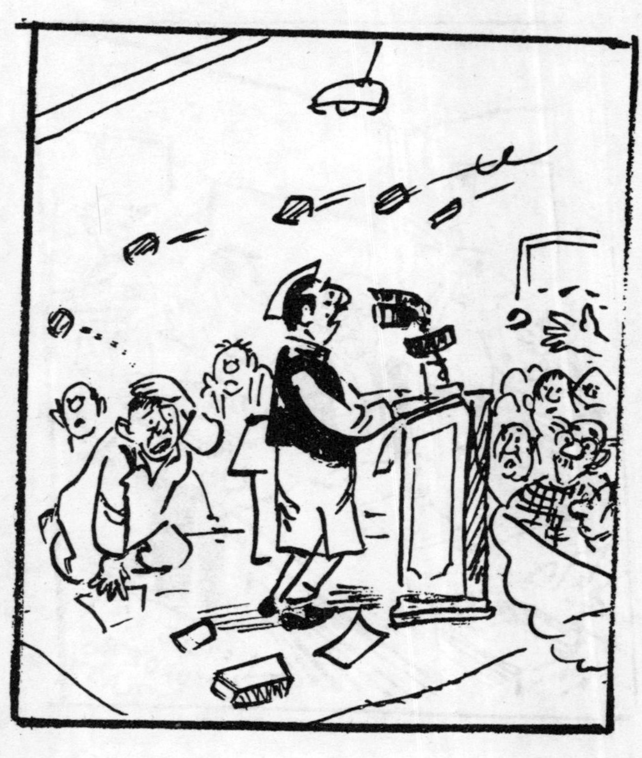

Now try telling them it's not your personal view but the official view.

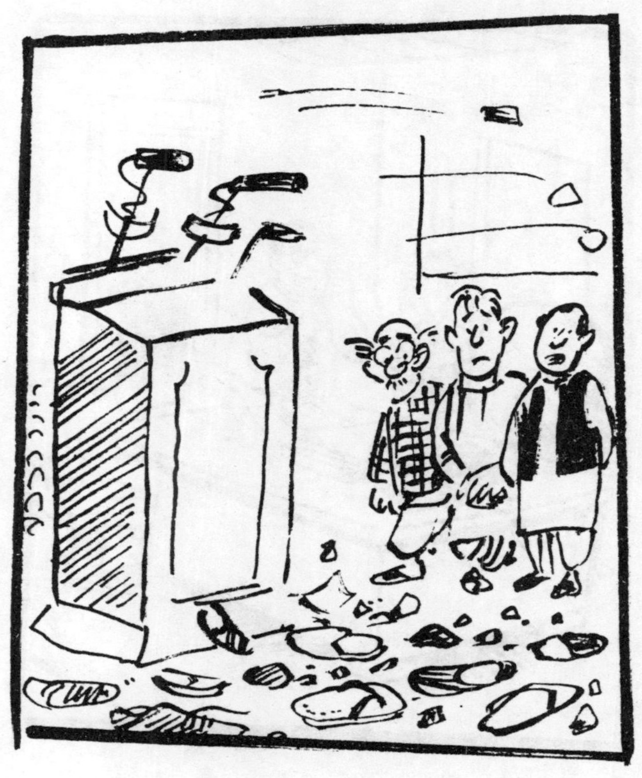

Don't feel bad about it, sir. Not all of them have thrown slippers. Quite a few seem to be friendly. They have hurled only stones.

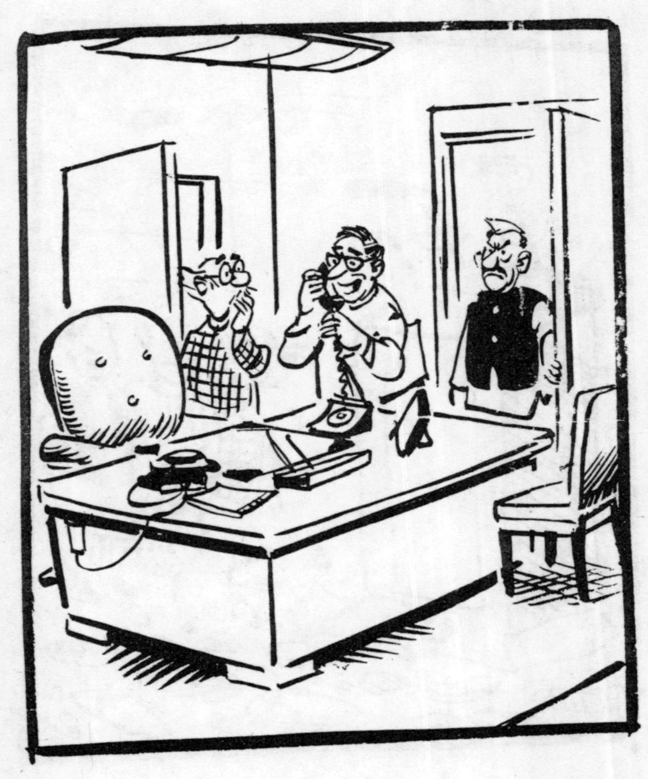

...and for god's sake, don't quote me...!

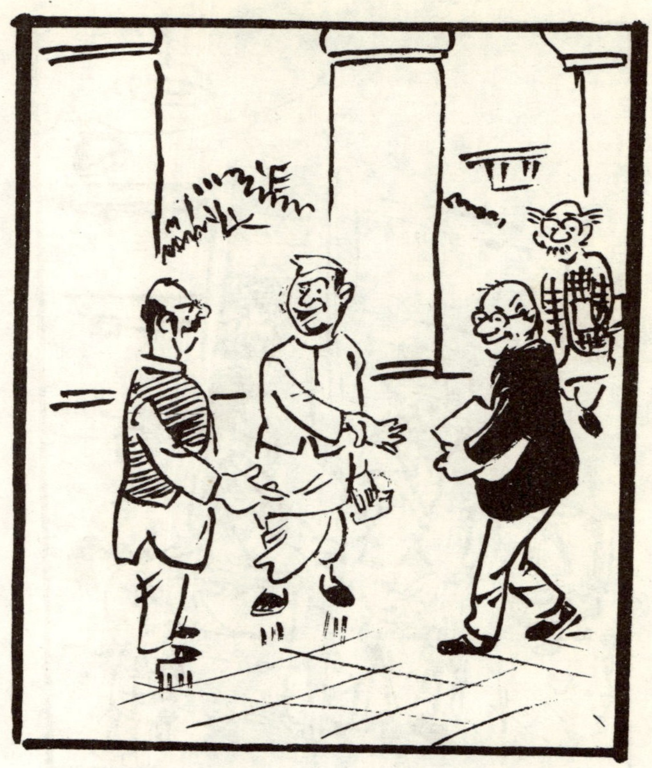

Meet my lawyer. He is very good. He is the one who saved me from that scam I was involved in. I suggest you take his help too.

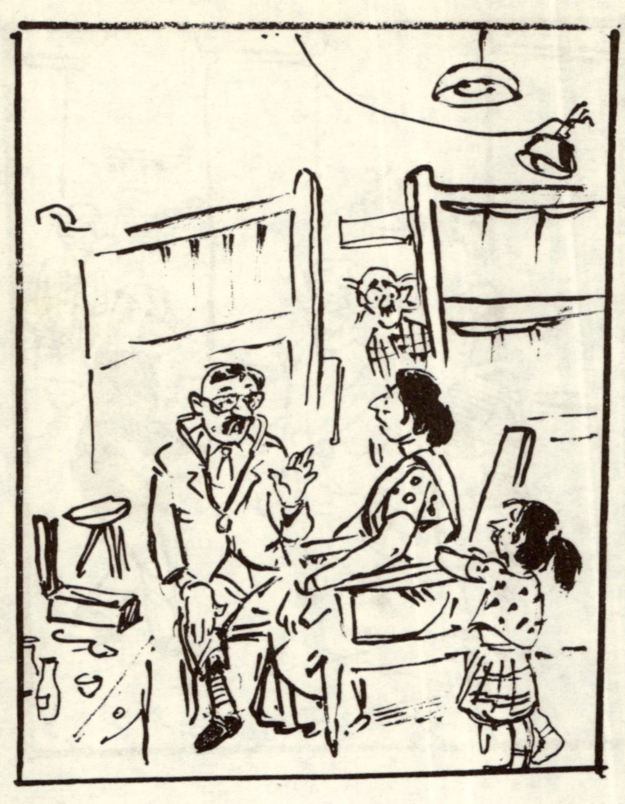

Nothing is really wrong. It's just that your blood pressure is a bit high. For some time stop helping your kid with her homework!

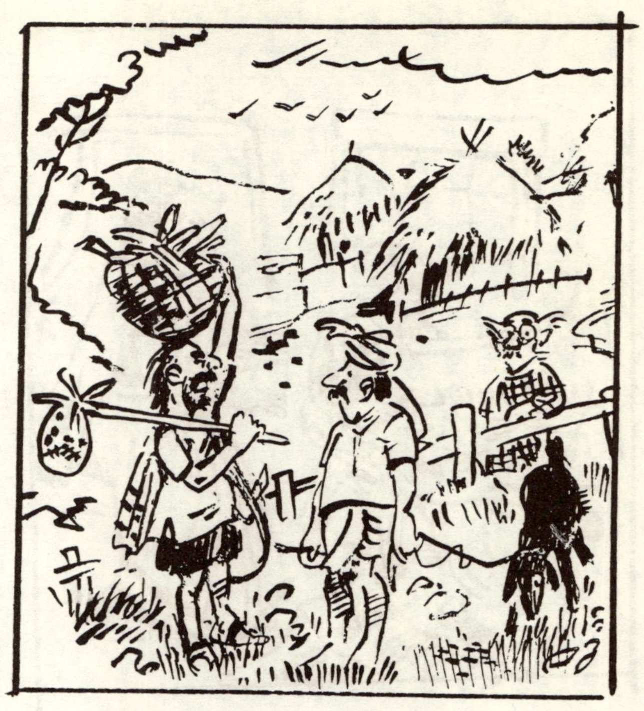

I went to the city to settle down there. It's impossible—
no water, no power, roads full of potholes, dirty. So I
changed my mind and have come back.

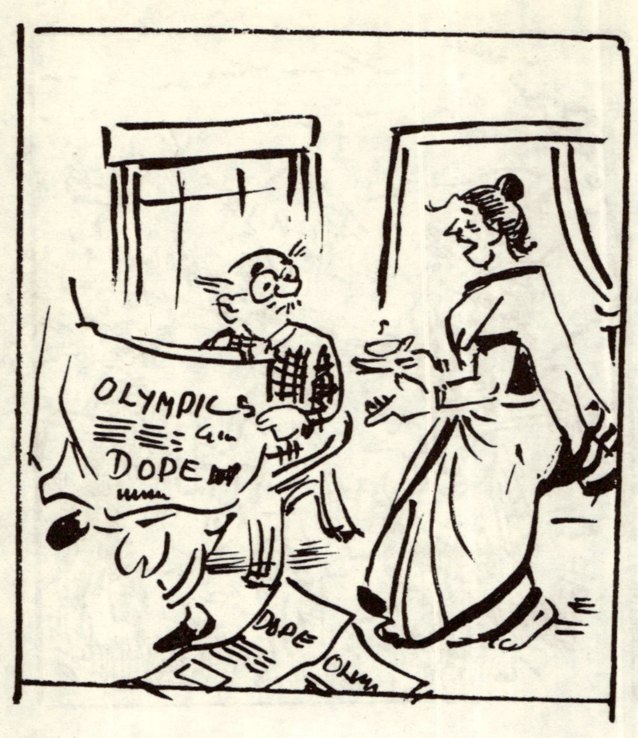

If this dope is really that good and enhances efficiency and performance, then why shouldn't our politicians and ministers take it?

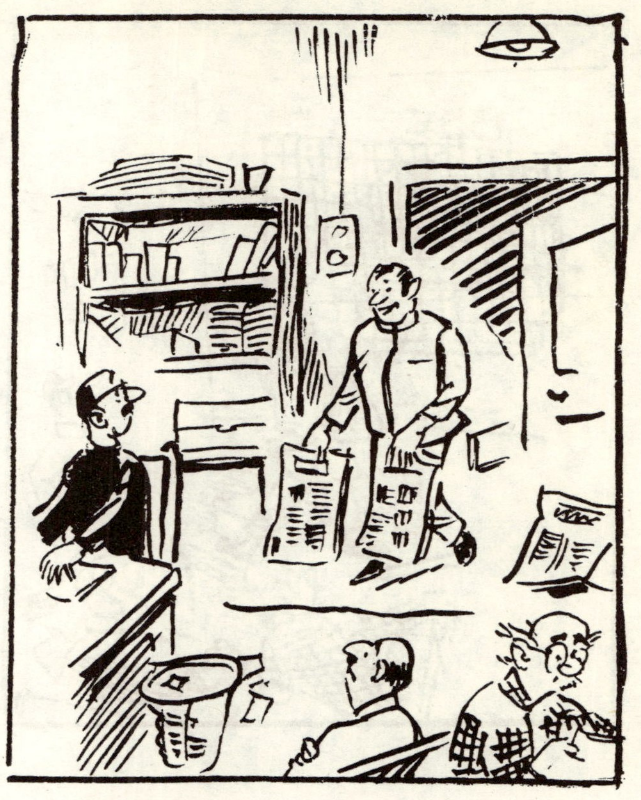

The media has misquoted and distorted your speech, sir. Let us not issue any correction. Actually, it reads very well now.

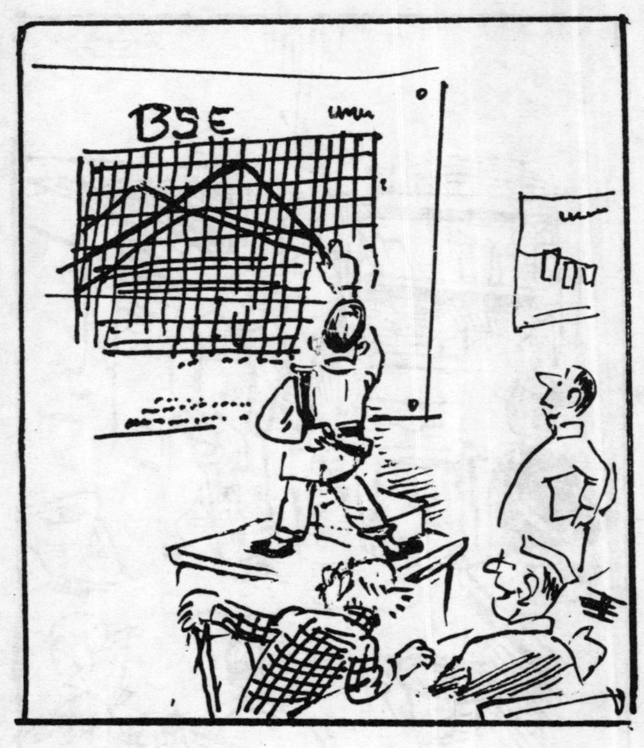

That peon is very intelligent. Every morning he corrects the graph himself without my telling him!

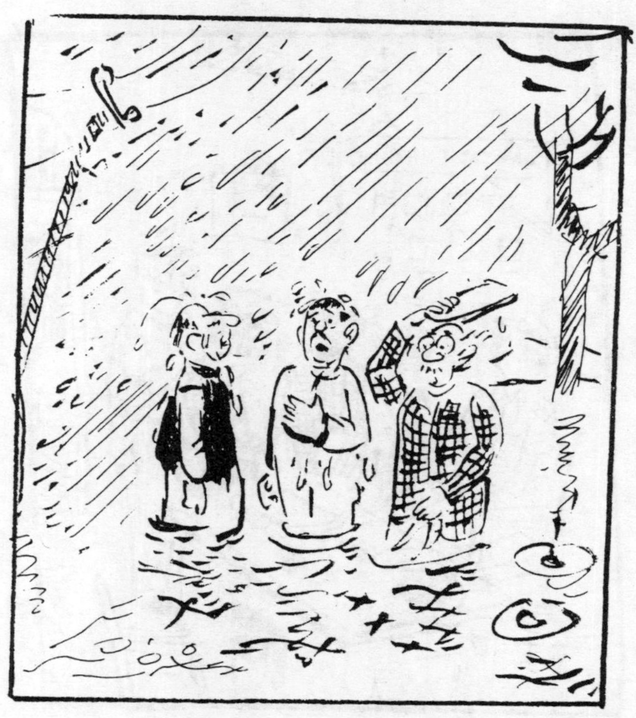

Sorry, sir, I didn't bring the umbrella because you are touring the drought-affected regions and the weather forecast also said the dry spell will continue.

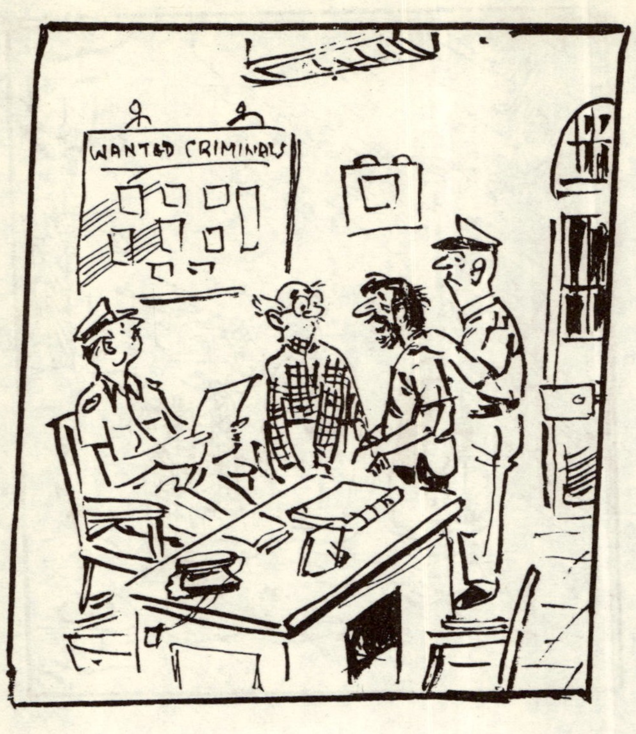

I went underground to avoid arrest. But there it is so overcrowded, I decided to come up and surrender, sir.

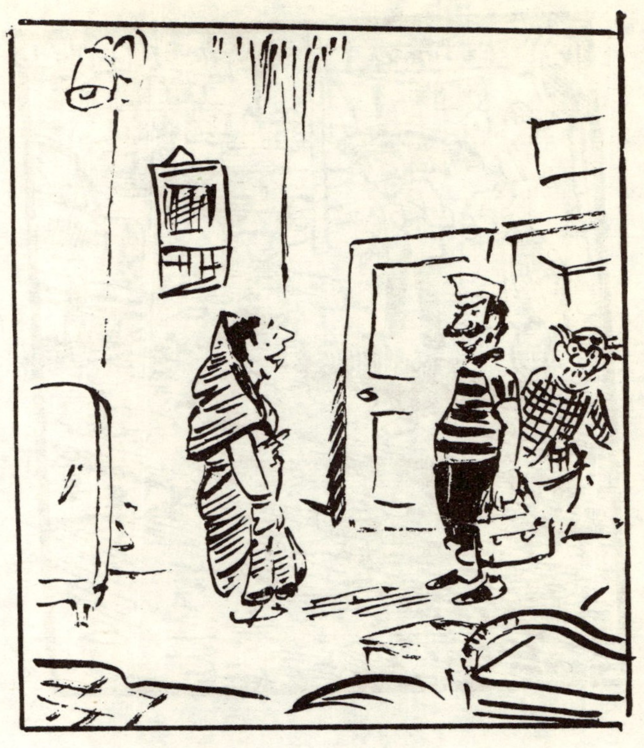

*I heard the good news that you can continue to be a
minister till you are proven guilty! Is that true?*

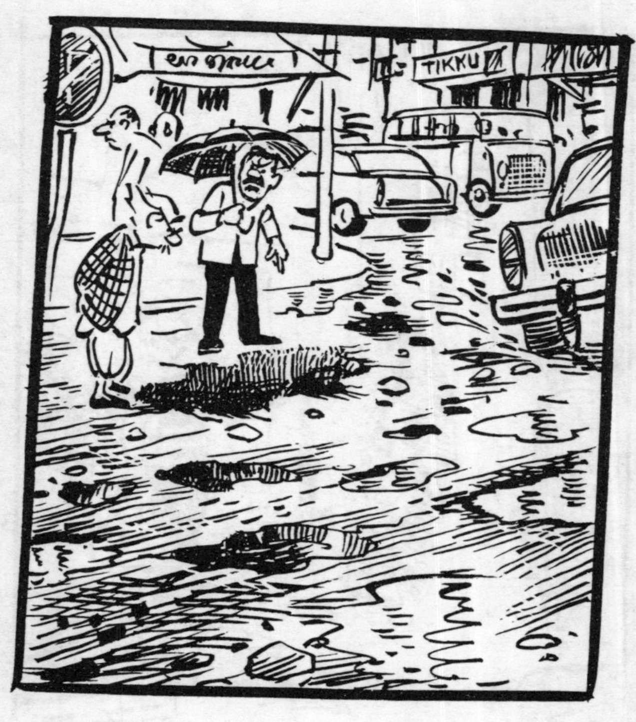

Look, a Maruti! I knew this was bound to happen the way they maintain the roads these days!

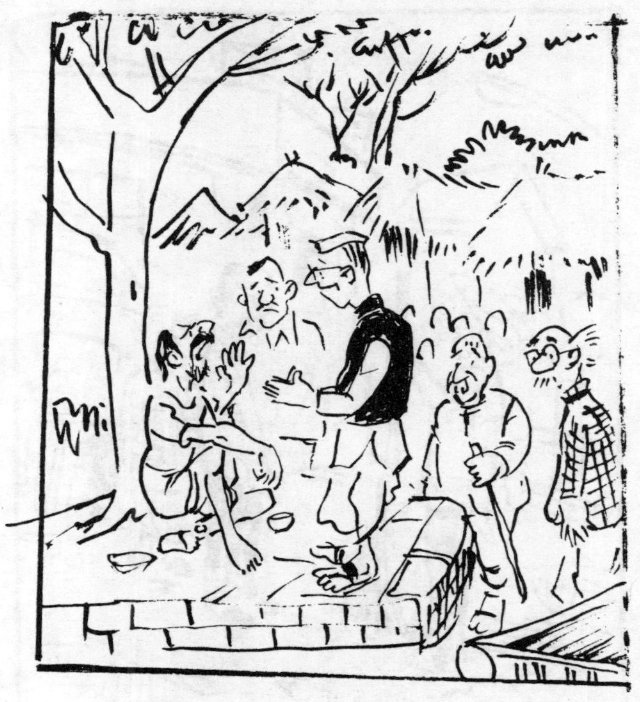

*Please, sir. No need to plead with me to give up fasting.
I am not fasting. I'm starving... like so many others in
this village.*

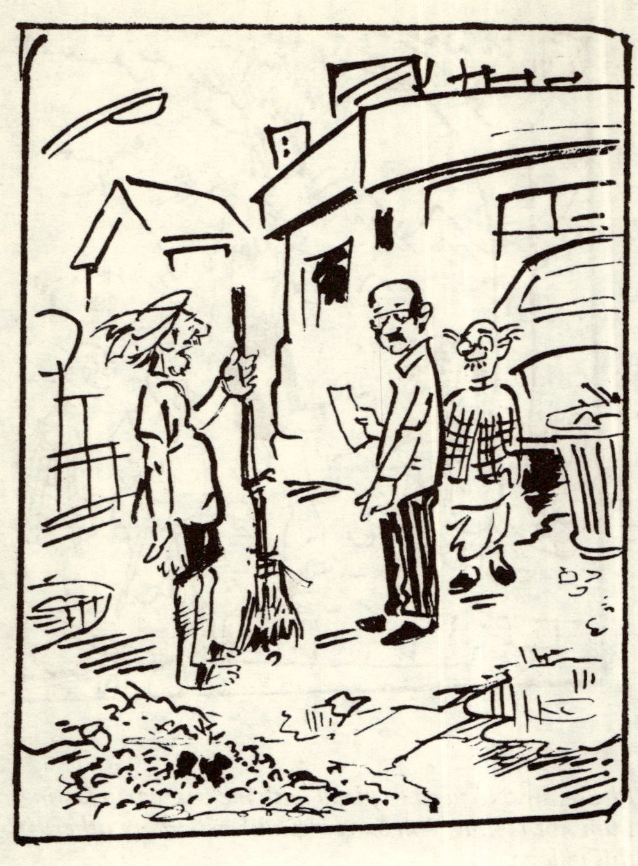

No, *sir. I have not swept it, because it was there even
before the municipal strike was declared and called off.*

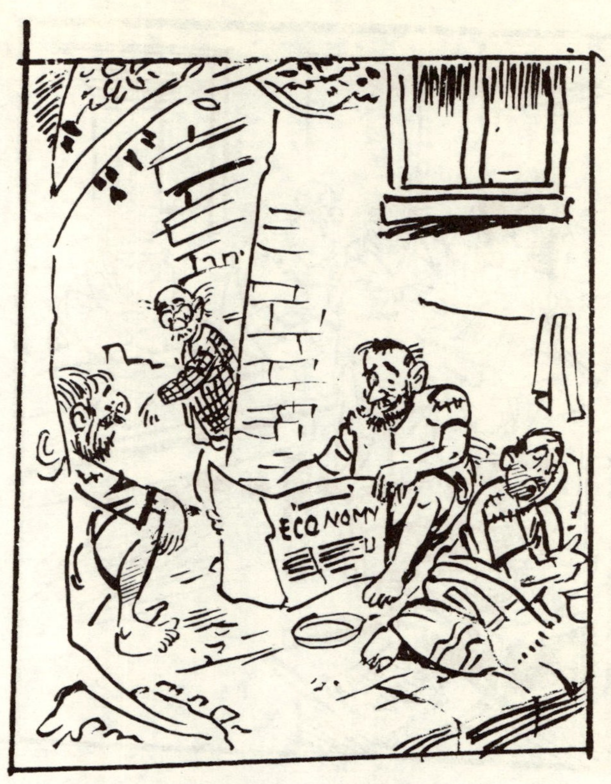

Terrific progress in growth rate, industry, exports, exchange reserve... What a change from the miserable situation we were in!

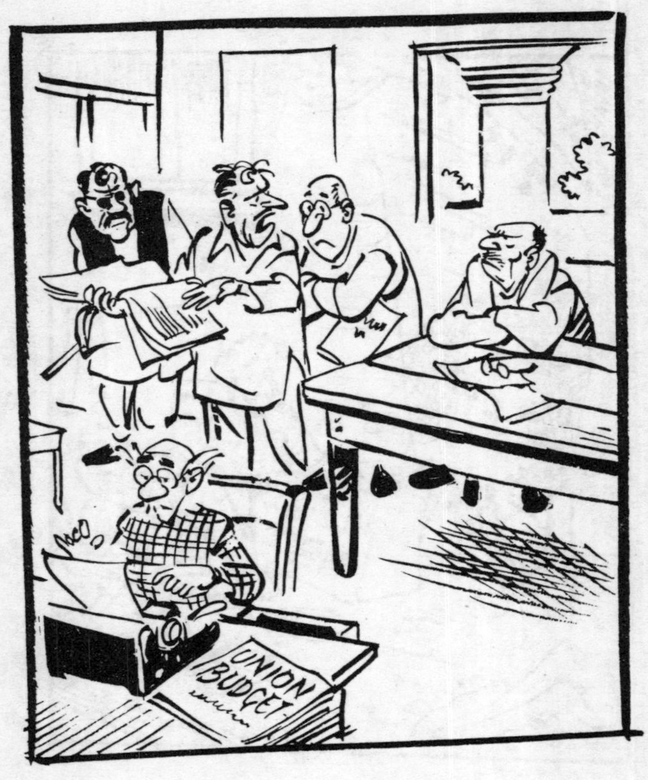

Maybe it's a good budget economically. But we must vote against it—politically, it's an attempt to destroy the Opposition!

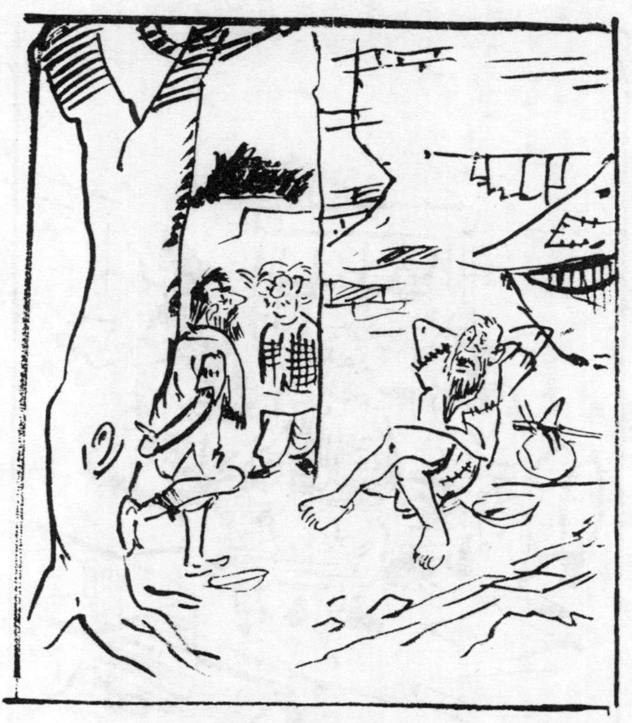

You may think so. But I feel this year's budget is the
best I have seen in all these years!

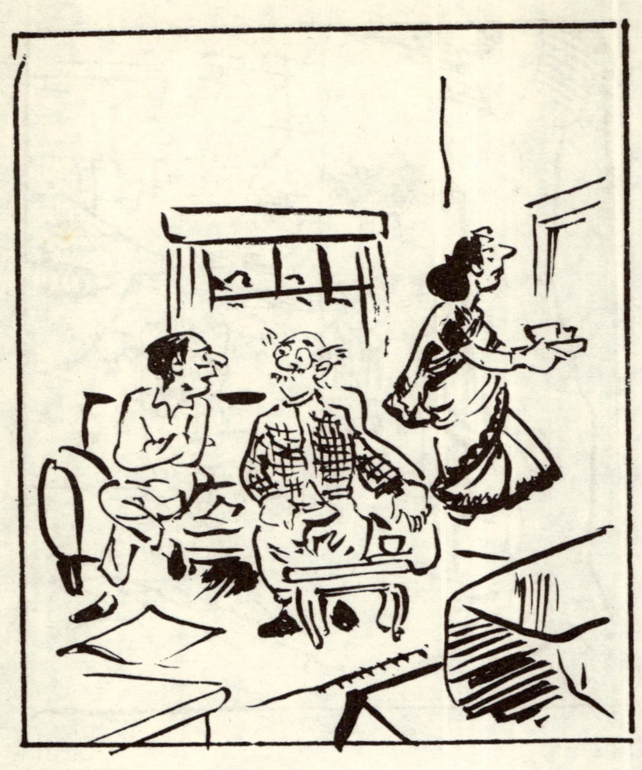

I can't understand what she says. Too much of the budget reports and analysis has affected her. She says we must cut down on BV and CO and hike the salary of MS and C, and so on... all the time.

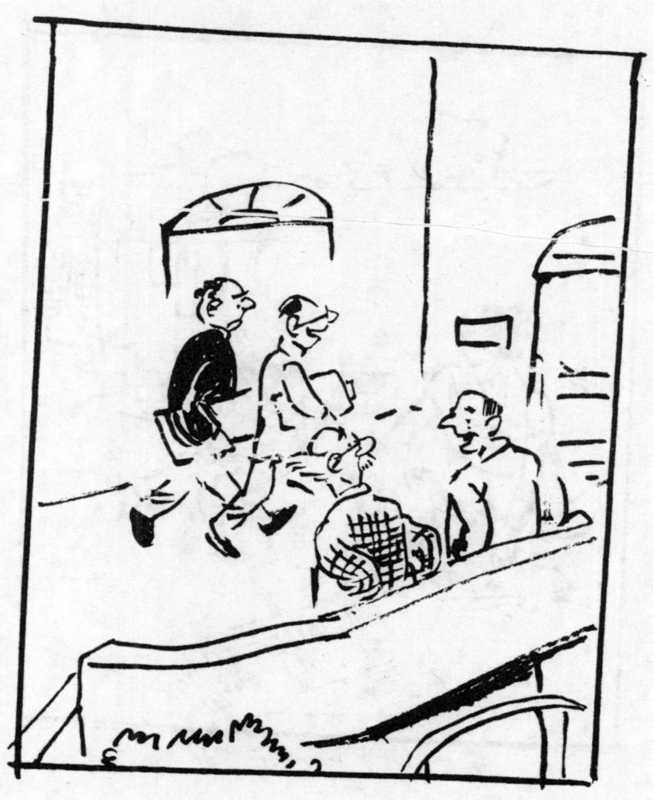

No, the one grinning and laughing is the finance minister.
The one with a grim, frowning look is an economic
expert!

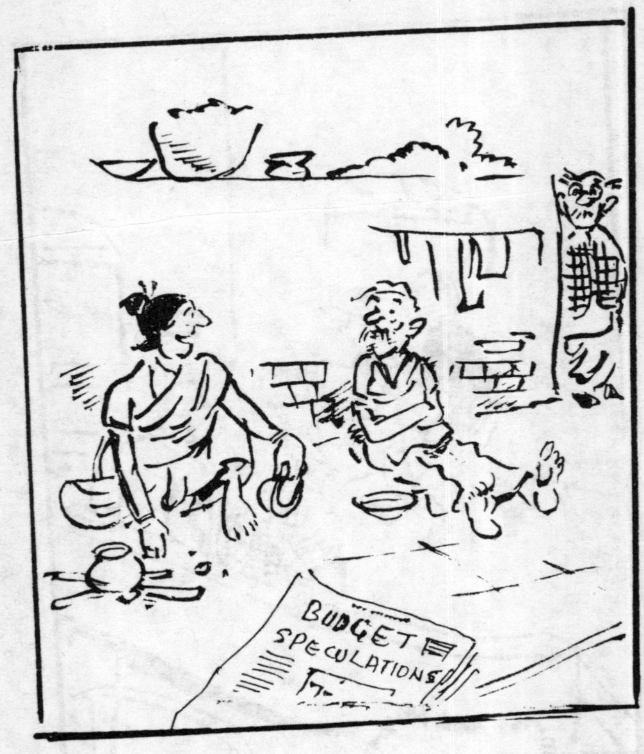

Nice to see you relaxed and happy. Those days when you had a job and income, you used to be a nervous wreck at the time of the annual budget!

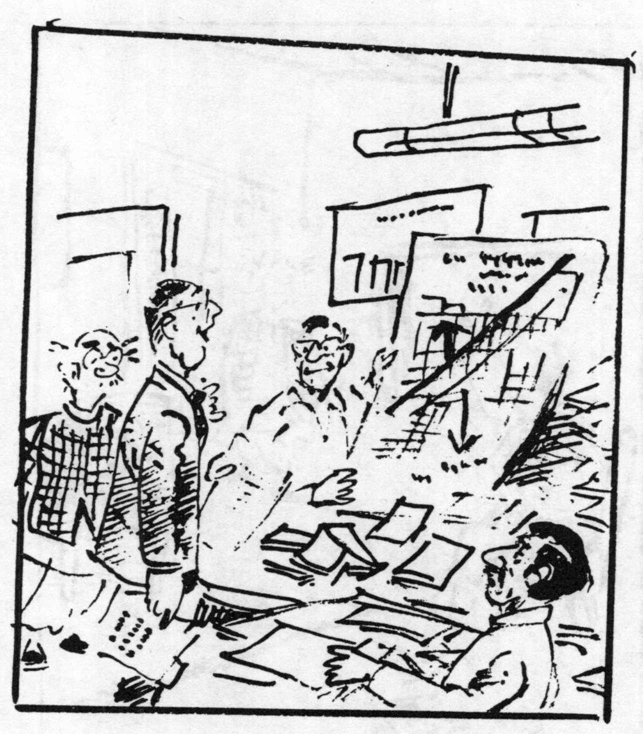

Excellent plan to provide water, electricity and other facilities for those living under the poverty line. But we must do something to give these to those living above the poverty line, in the cities...

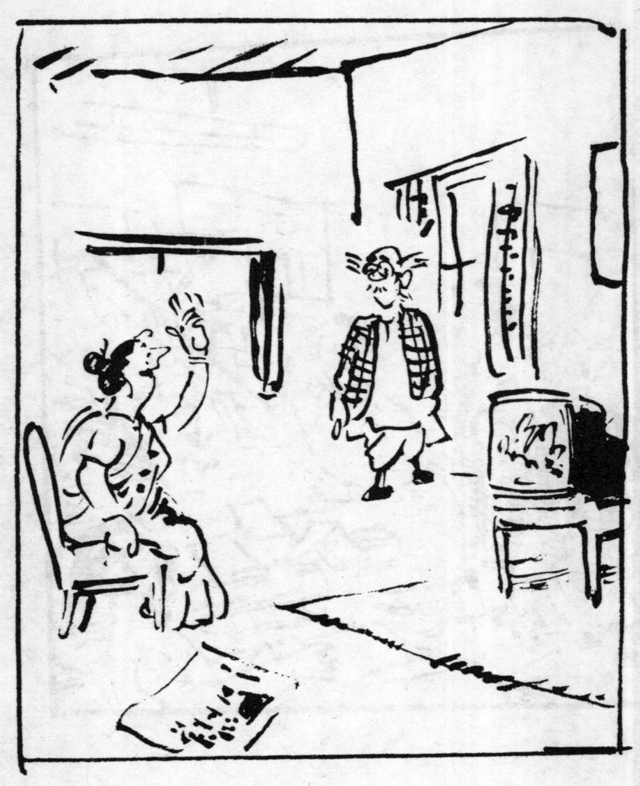

Come, let's watch. After a long time they are showing something which has nothing to do with the budget!

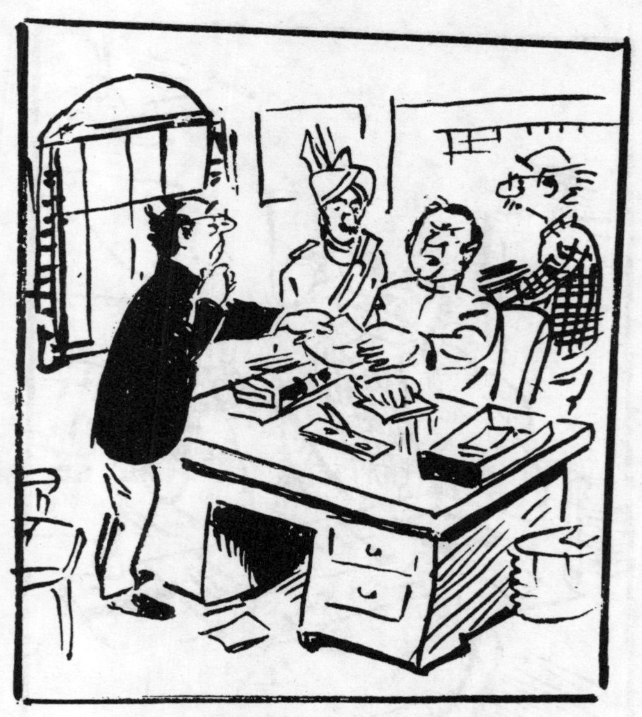

Don't waste my time. Make up your mind quick! You want to give your resignation or withdraw it?

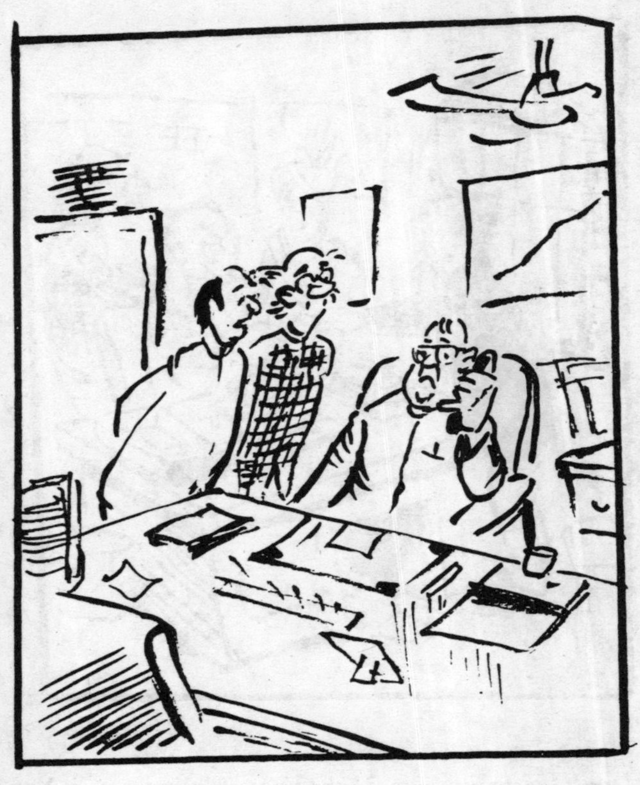

Sorry to interrupt you, sir. Whatever instructions and orders you are giving are of no use. You are talking on your spectacle case, not on your cellphone!

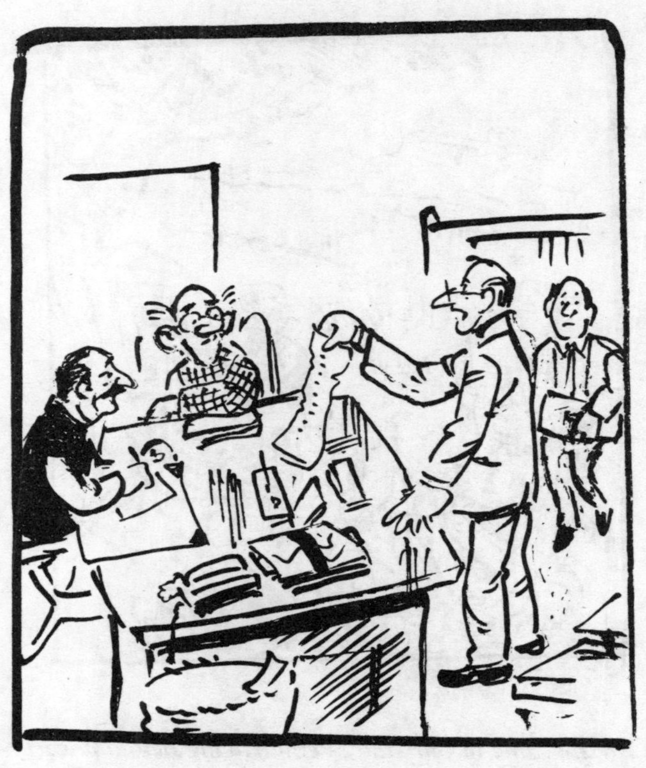

You wanted some points for discussion with the visiting Pakistan minister. Here they are, sir; they have been jotted down years ago and used repeatedly over the years without any change...

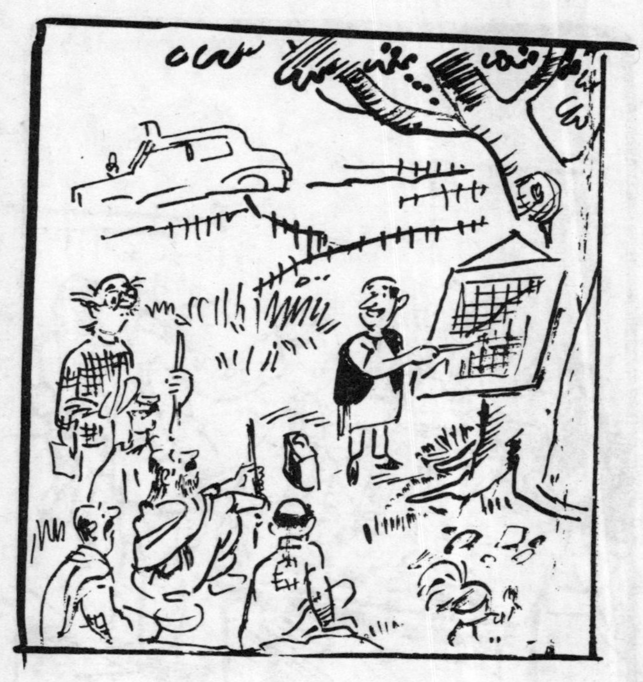

All are same in our state. People living below poverty line suffer from lack of food, shelter, water, jobs etc. Those living above it suffer from power cut, load-shedding, water shortage, scams etc.

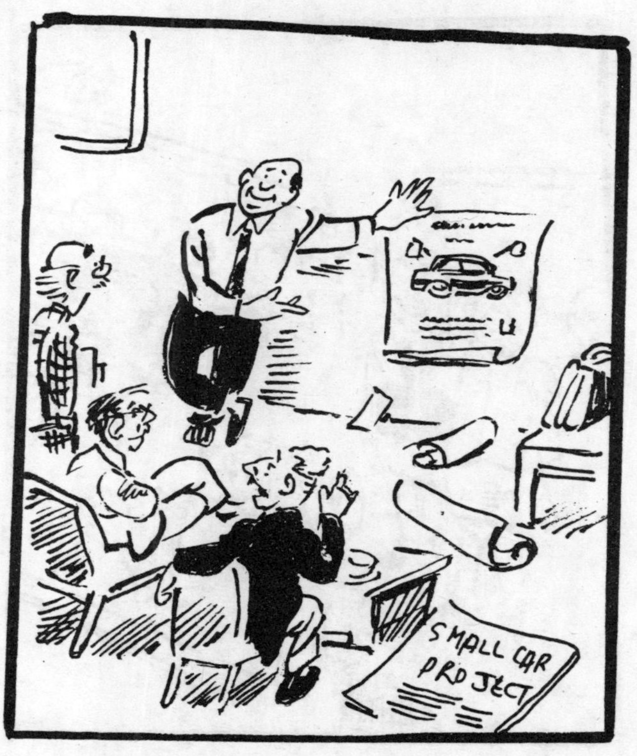

The manufacturer has designed the small car, sir. He says it has to be just the size shown in the picture, considering the city's parking problems, size of its roads, the traffic congestion etc.

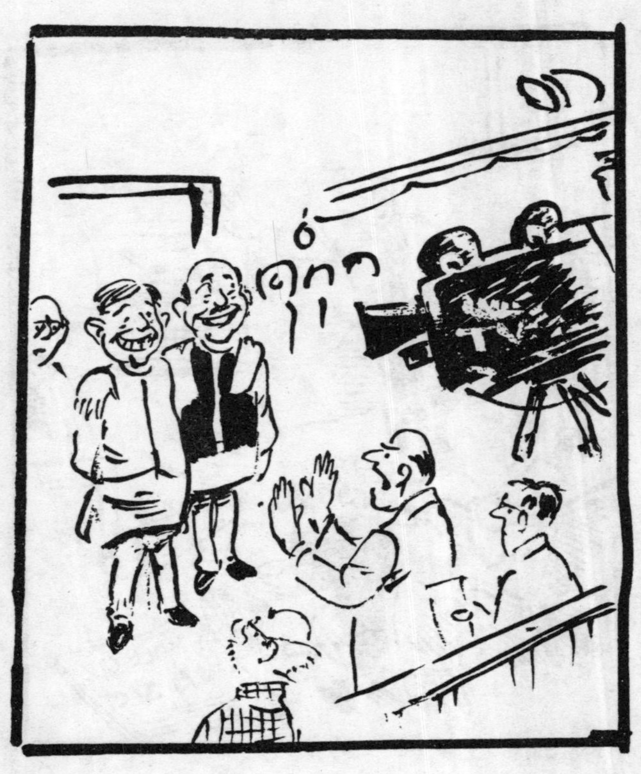

The state is facing a grave situation. Your talks have failed! Please stand apart; no grinning and no smiling, please!

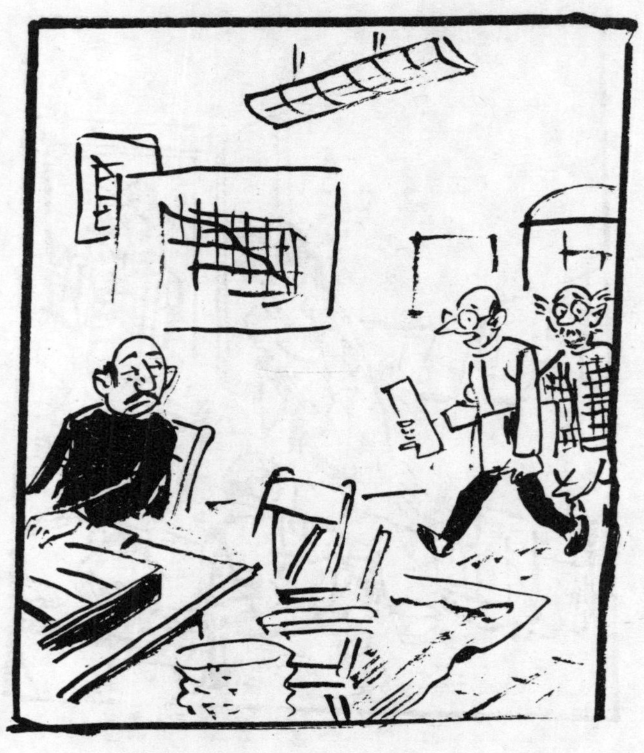

Better leave this problem alone, just as it has been all these years. If we try to solve it, it will lead to more complicated problems, sir.

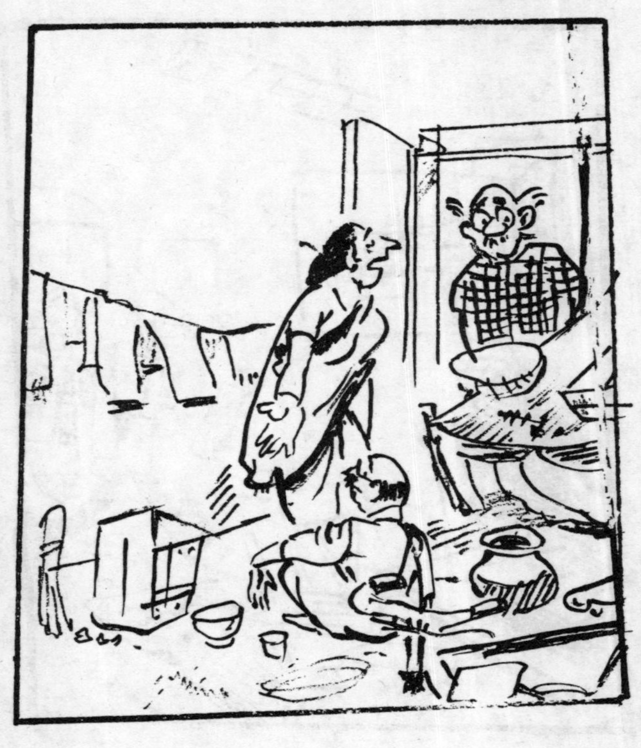

Everything is fine. It is just that he doesn't want to give the impression we are living beyond the known sources of our income, if any income-tax chap happens to walk in.

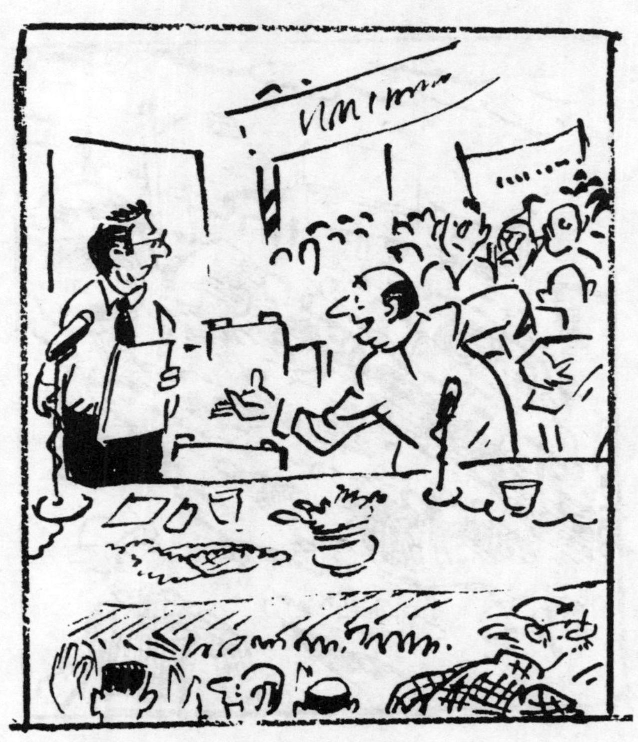

Excellent speech, sir. Please, may I have it? I'll read it out too.

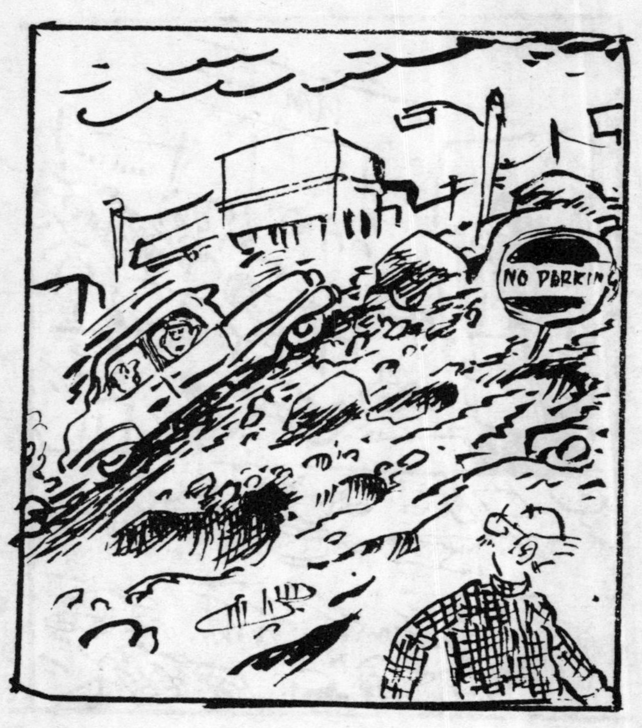

By the other road? No, sir, it is terrible. The municipal corporation has completely neglected it. It is impossible to drive on it!

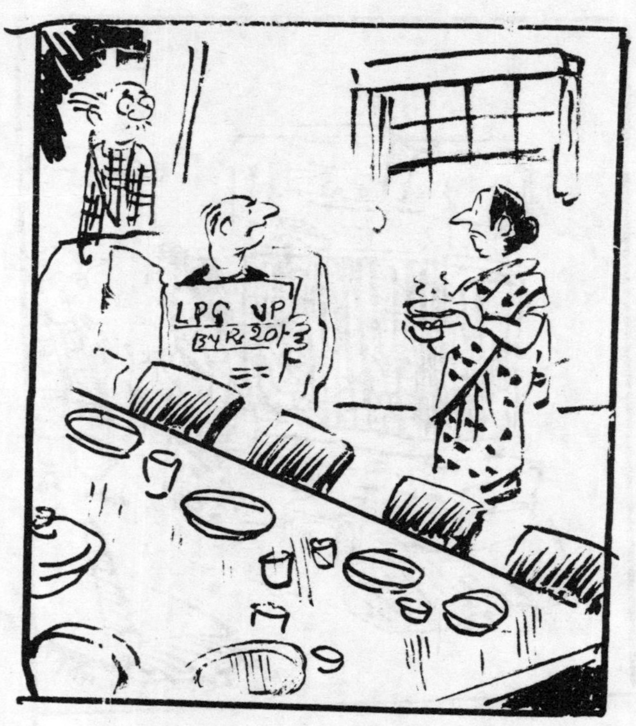

Look, I can't afford to provide both lunch and dinner every day. Just cook lunch one day and dinner the next day from now on!

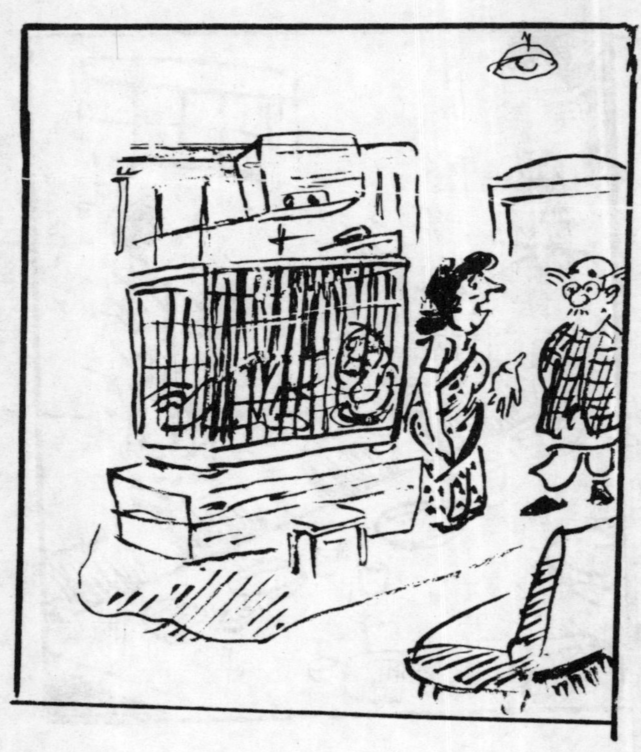

He sleeps like that these days. I told him panthers or leopards can't come into the city. But he says he has no trust in the authorities!

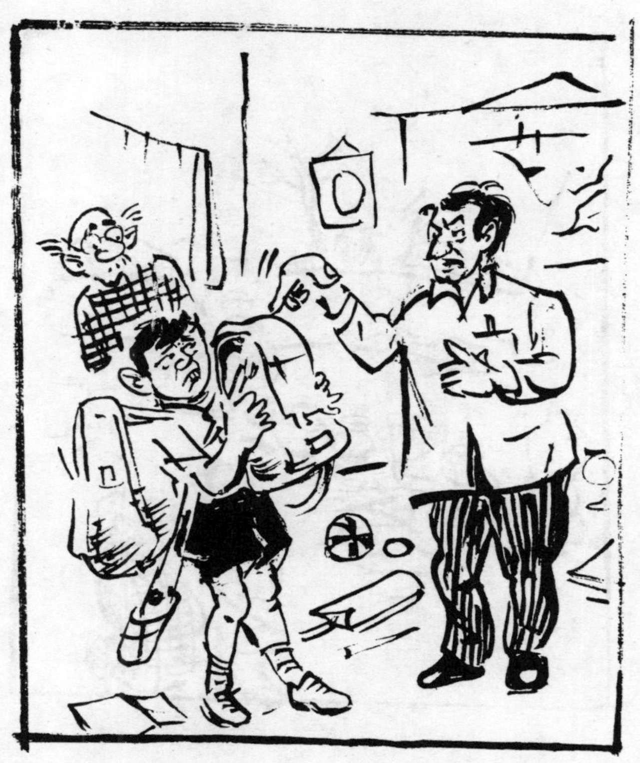

Now, remember, this contains your old textbooks and that one contains the revised editions. You have to read them both!

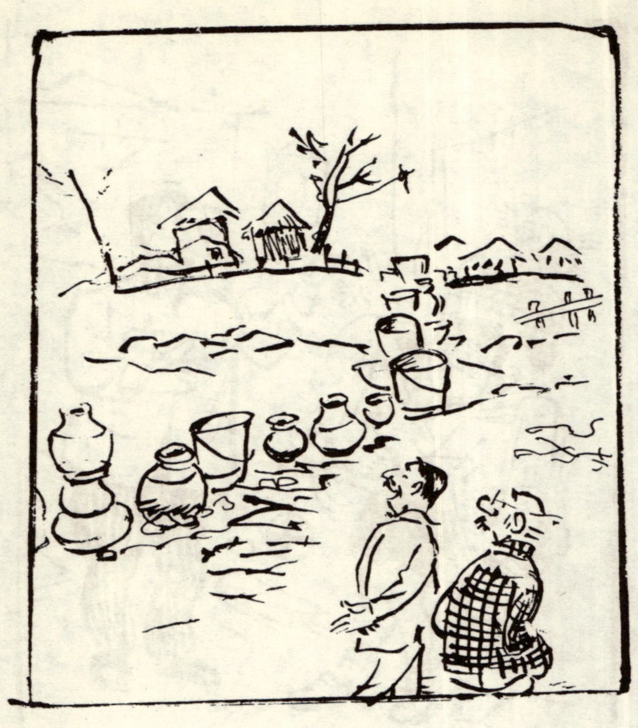

Not bad! One of the taps in the nearby village must be getting water!

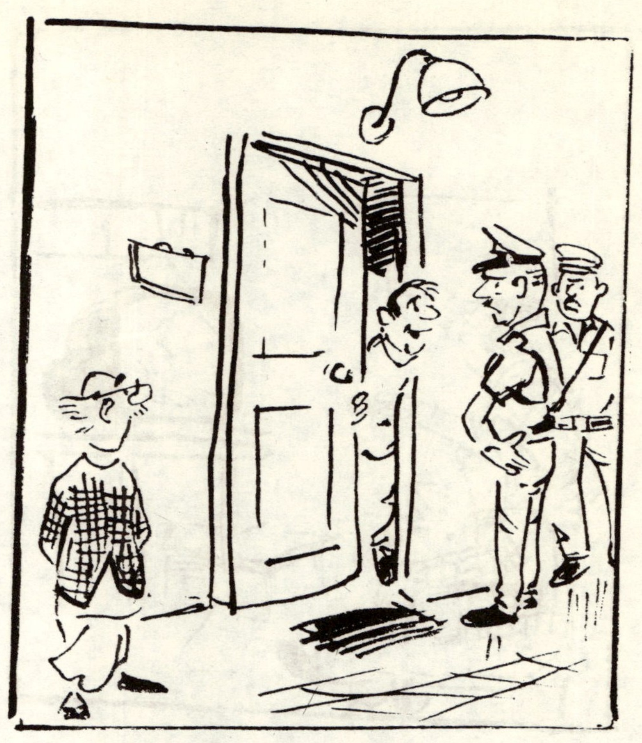

You have come to raid my house? But I've nothing to hide. Give me half-an-hour and then you can come in.

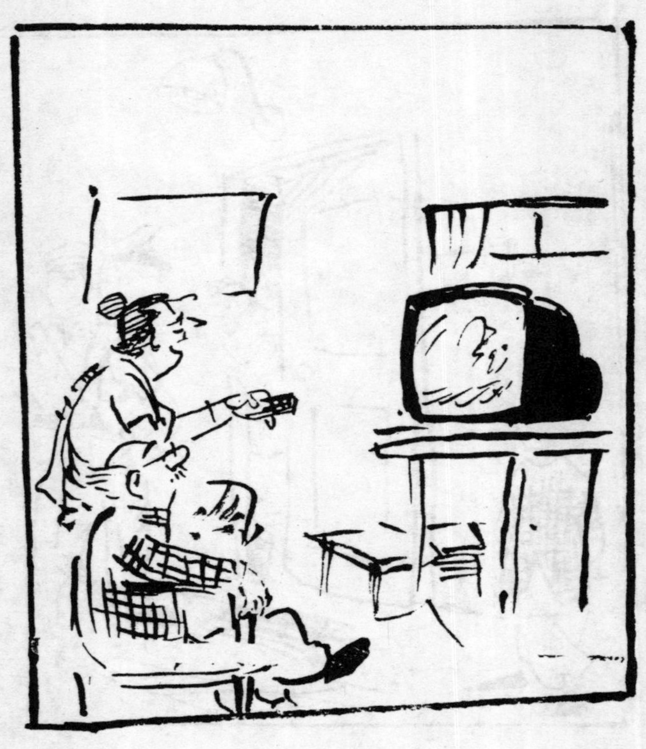

...violence, sex, murder, kidnapping, horror... just like in real life. What are TV and movies coming to!

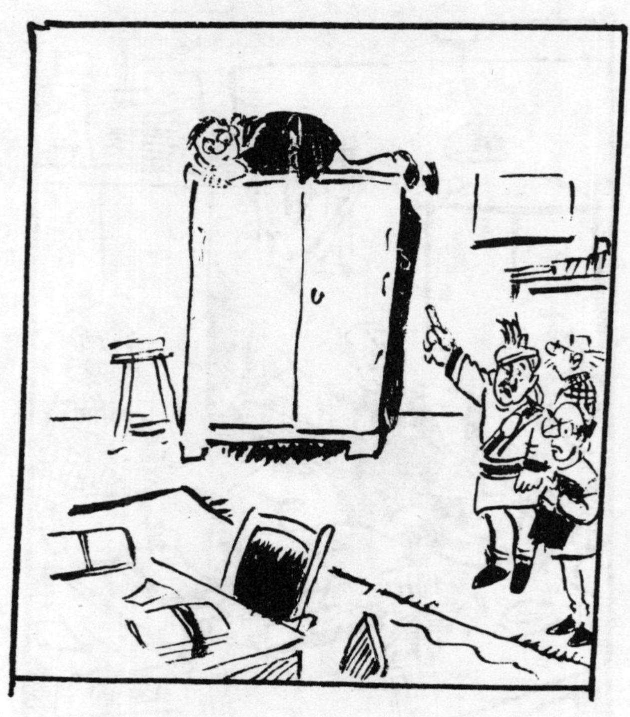

No, *he hasn't run away, sir. He is not that type. Look,* he is over there!

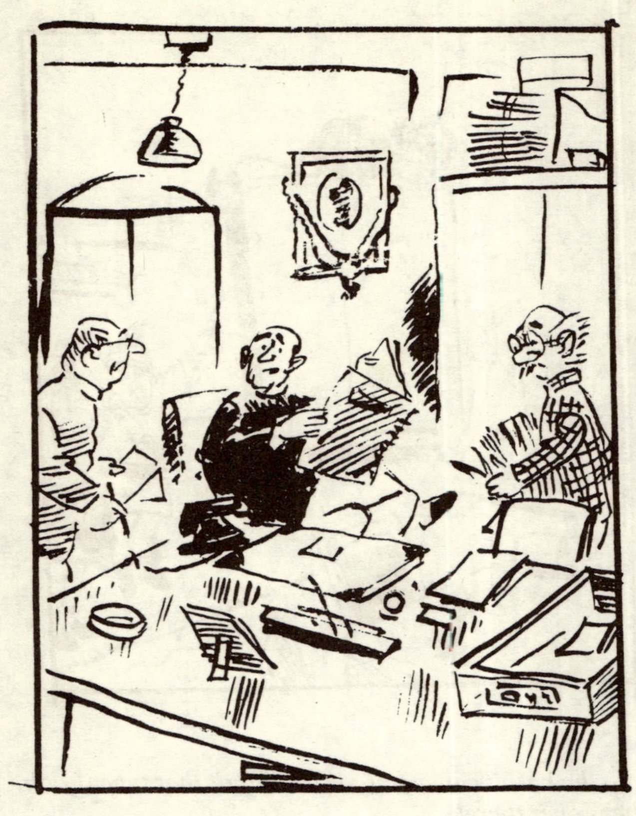

Find out what this means—'Report to TDC about CLT and get OK from NDC at once. Otherwise KRC will claim damages for PLC'!

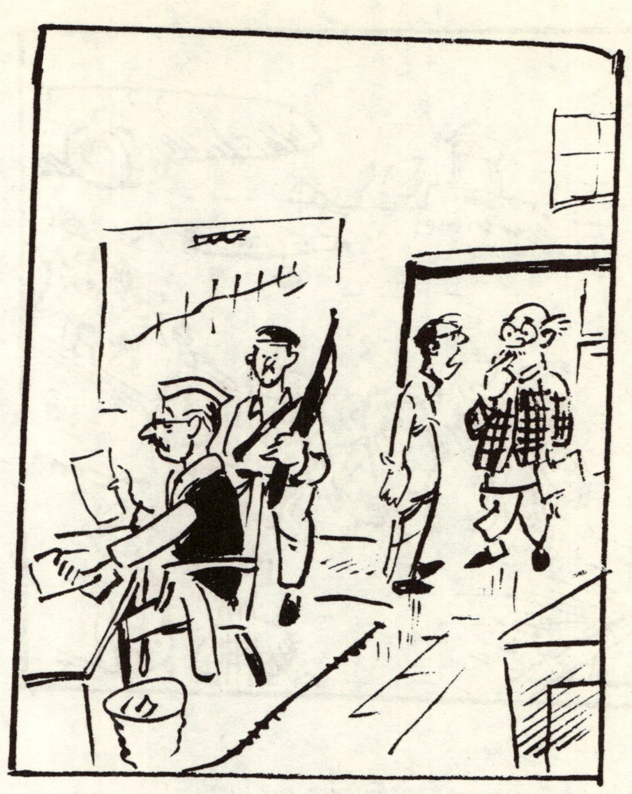

He wants to take a bold step. Instead of twelve security guards he wants only ten to surround him when he goes out!

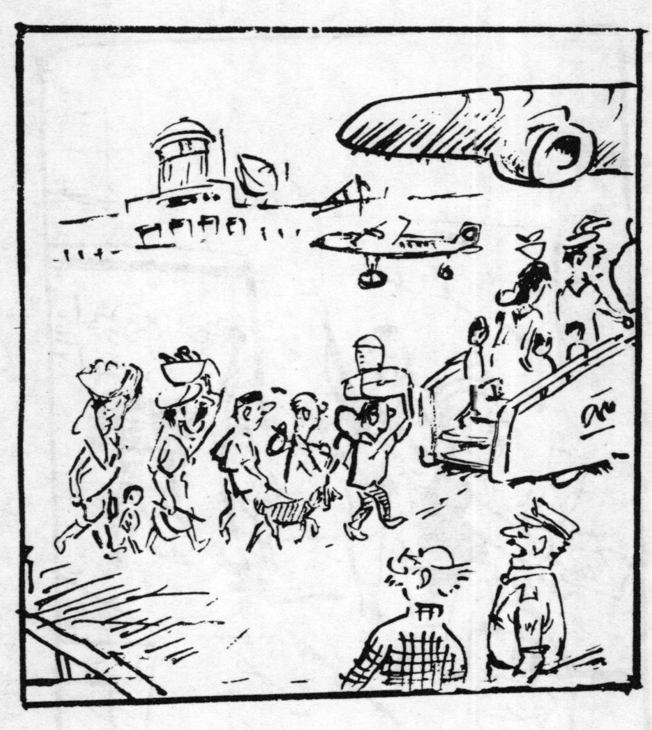

I hope they won't cut airfare any further!

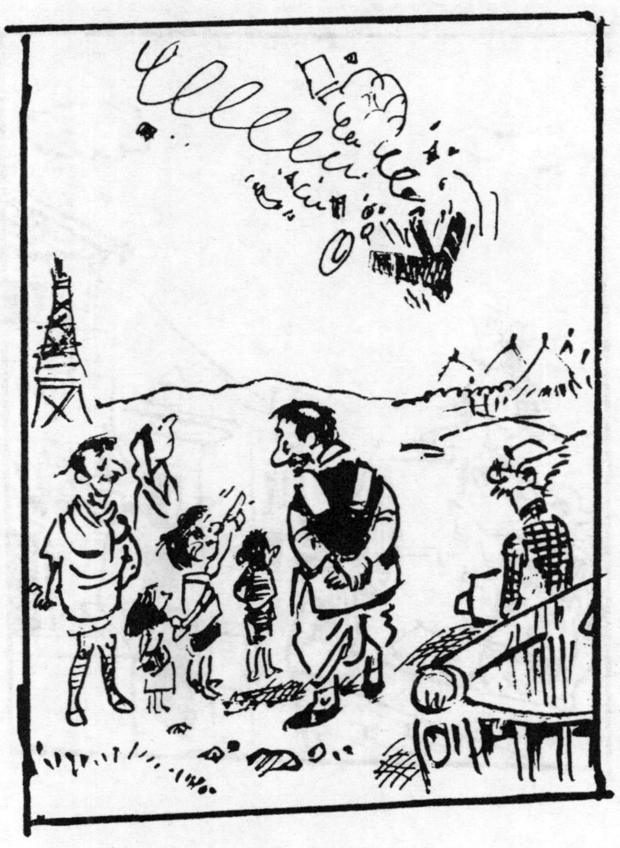

Kids around here seem to be extremely intelligent and well informed. This fellow is saying, 'Look, MIG-29... MIG-29... MIG...'!

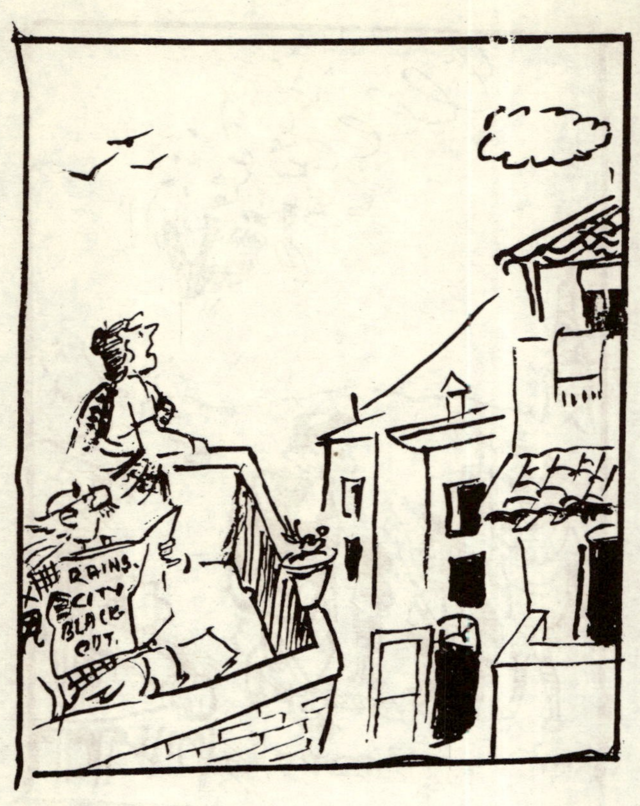

Better watch out... a patch of cloud is heading this way again. There might be a power cut and we will be plunged in darkness for hours!

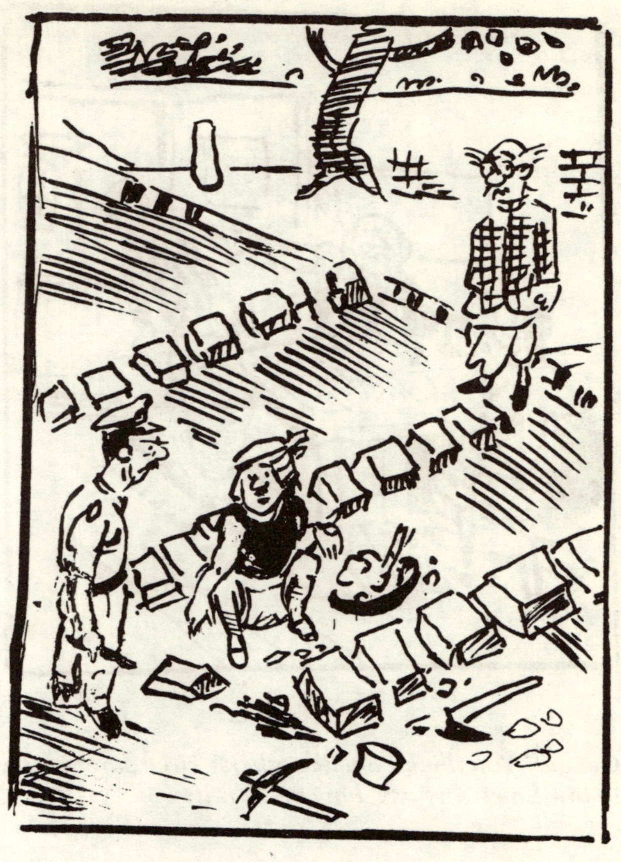

A *traffic policeman on duty here told me to put the*
road-dividers this way. It will prevent traffic jam as well
as traffic, he said.

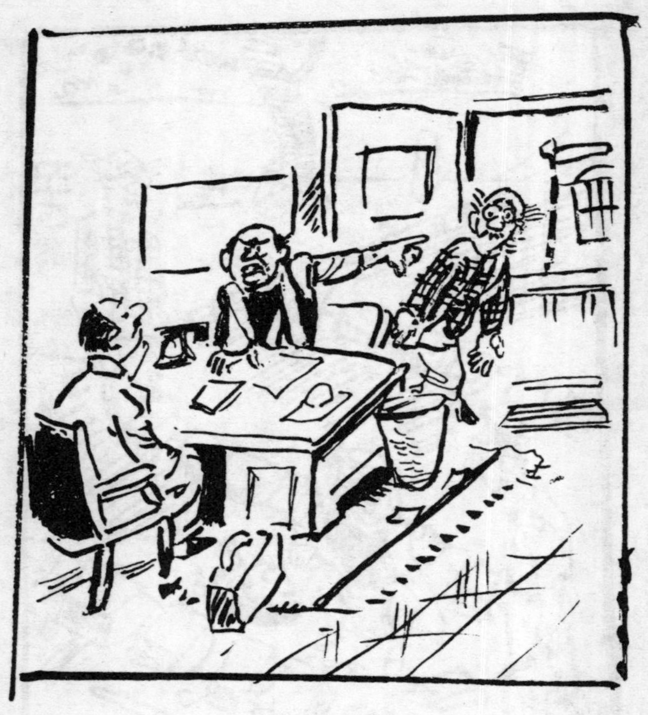

Get out! You think I am like others? How dare you try to bribe me? Anyway, how much is it?

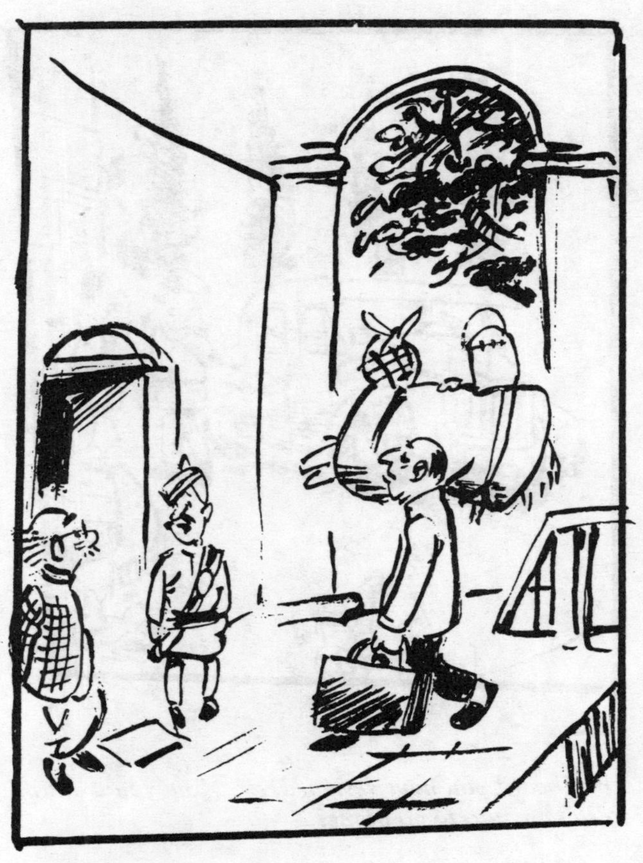

He comes prepared for quick transfer. You never can say these days when you will be ordered to move out!

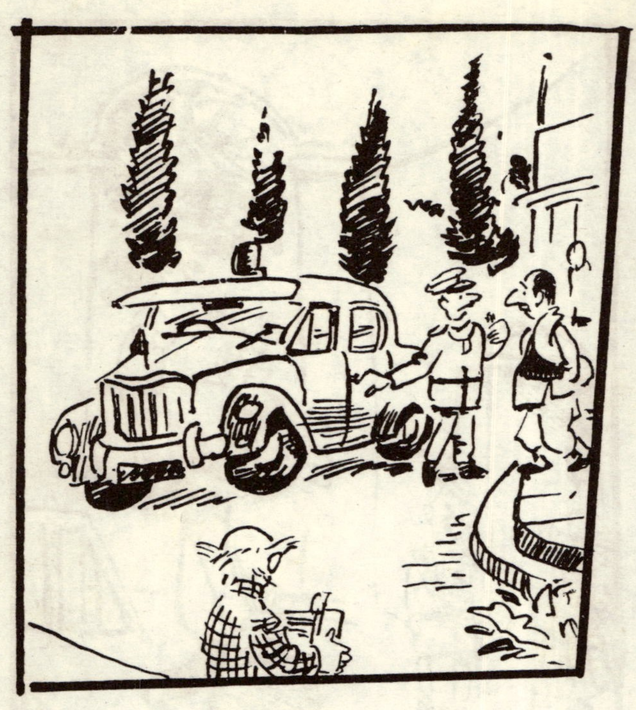

I just heard you have resigned, sir. Now you want me to call an auto to go home?

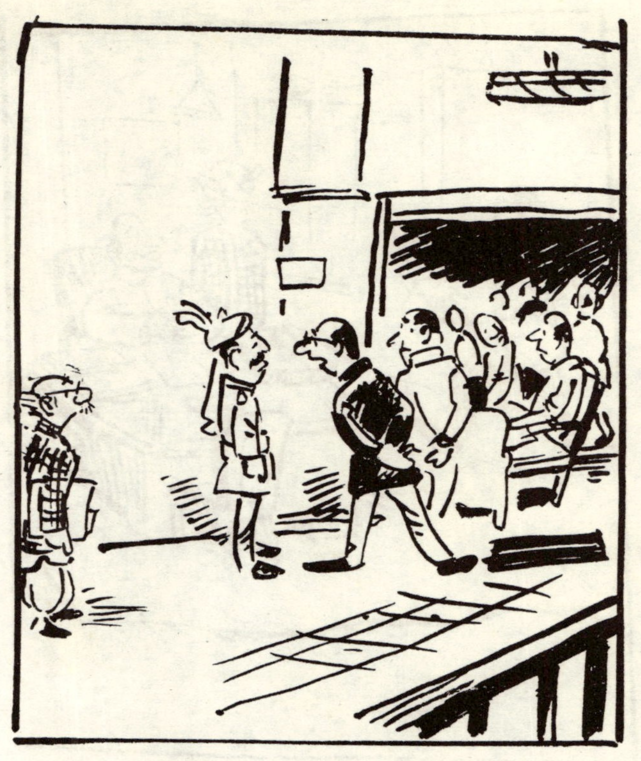

He wants to know what bilateral talks mean. Go, find out, quick! The talks begin in another ten minutes!

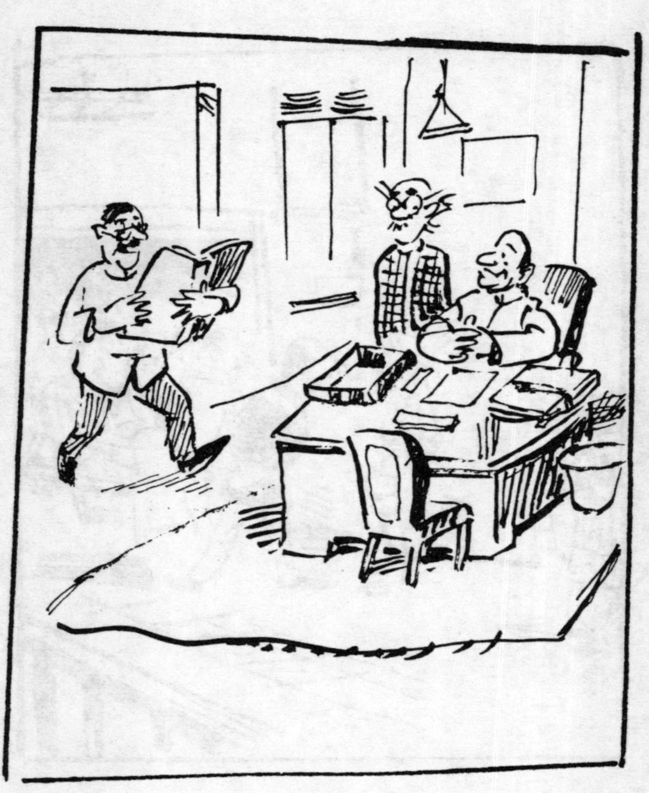

The investigation report has come, sir. This looting, murder, bomb blast, bus burning are all the work of the terrorists, sir, to disrupt normal life... just as you had guessed!

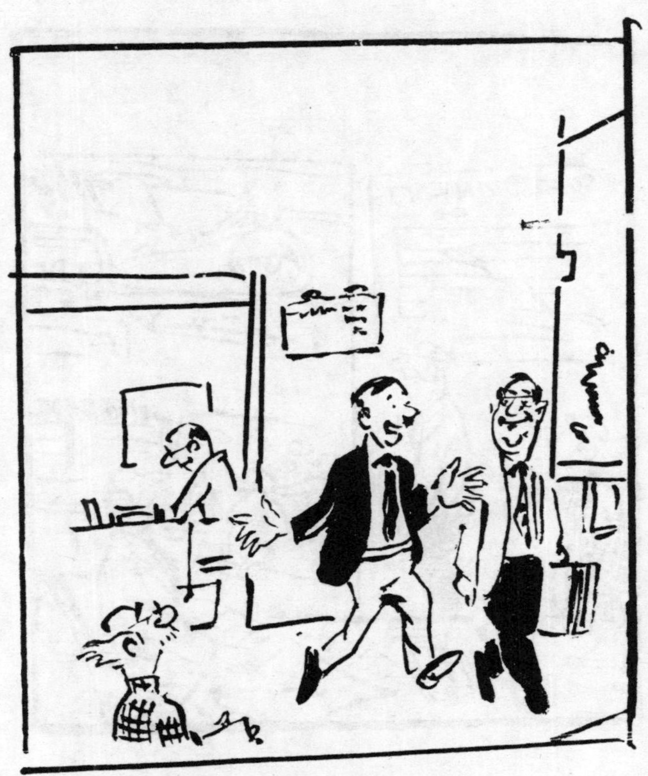

I am all for getting rid of corruption completely. But then after that how are you going to get things done?

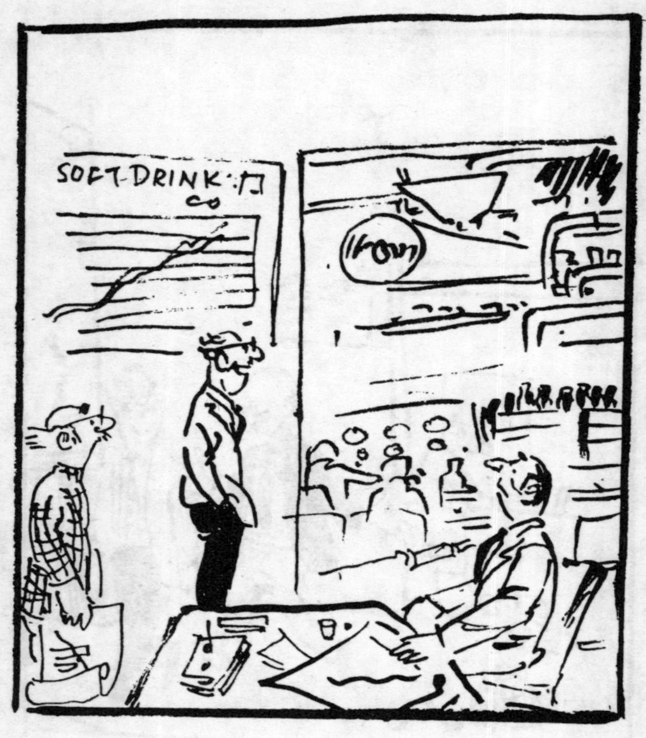

Ever since we put the mandatory notice on the bottles about the pesticide content in our product, the sales have gone up! The farmers are buying our product in bulk for spraying their crops with our soft drink!

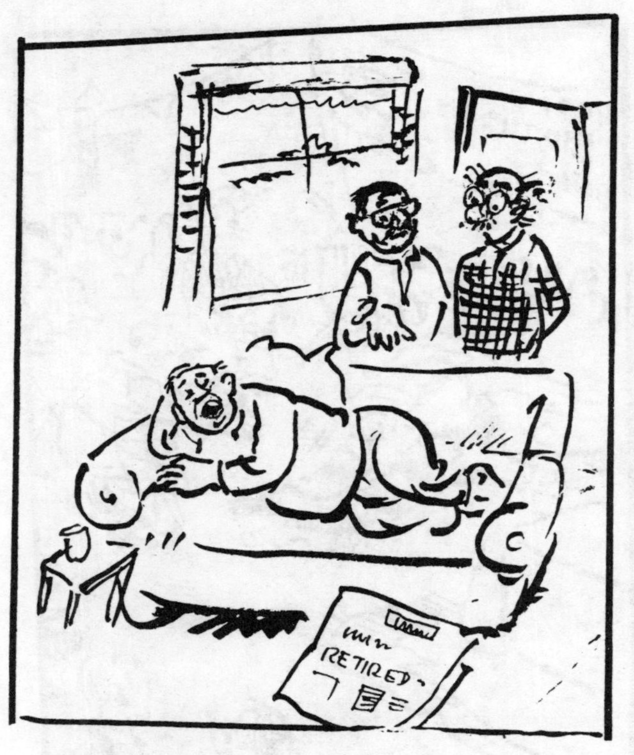

He became tired of politics and retired. Now he is busy doing social work—village upliftment, poverty eradication and so on!

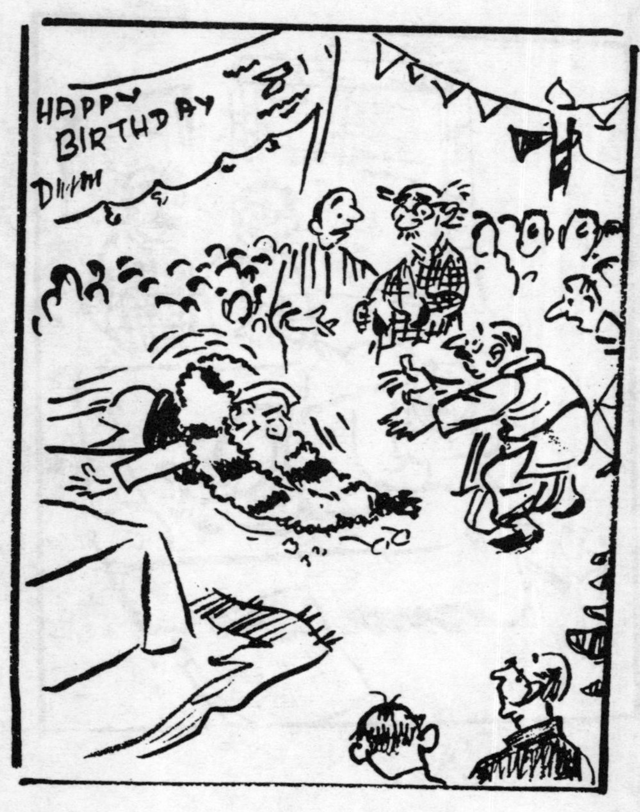

I told him to make the garland smaller... He is a frail old man and wouldn't be able to stand the weight of such a huge garland!

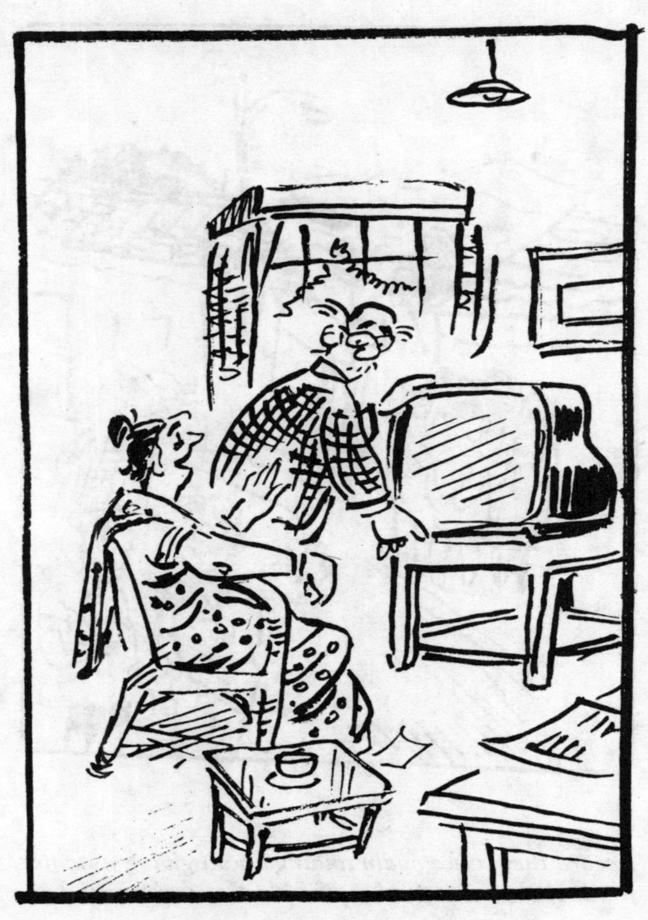

No, *no*, don't switch it on. I prefer watching it as it is
rather than the programmes they are showing these days!

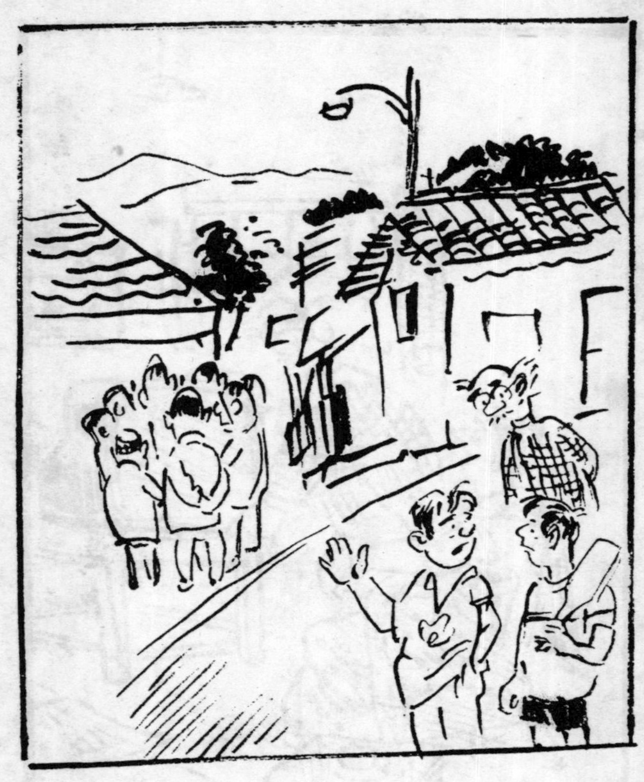

I heard them once again talking about giving us water, food, shelter... I think some elections are round the corner.

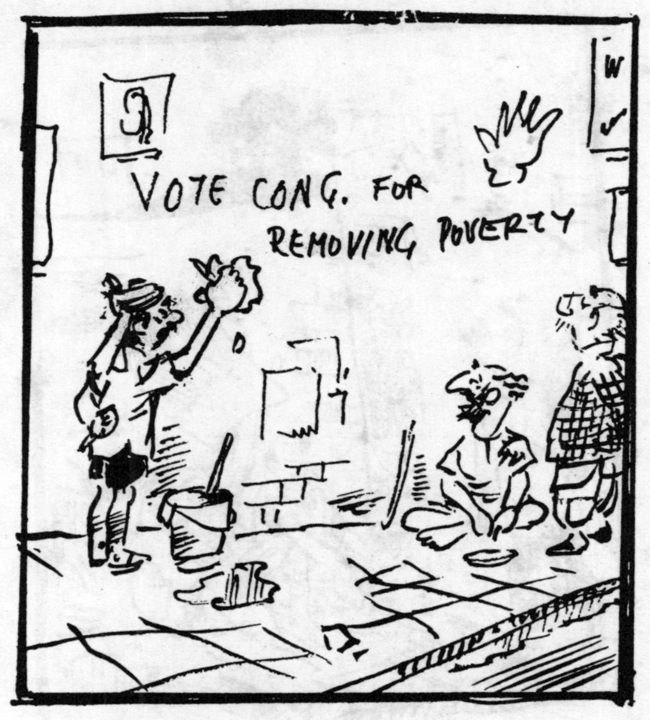

Don't wipe it out. It will be useful during the next elections!

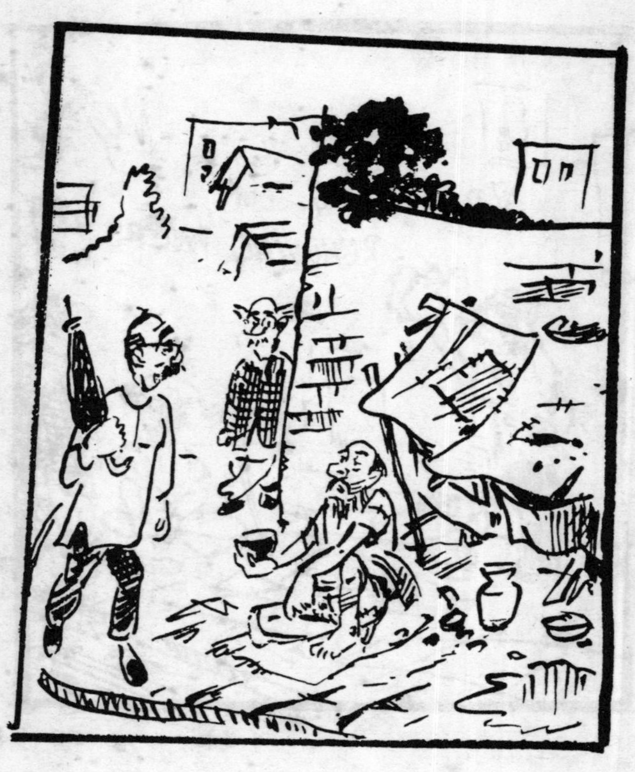

Thanks, for wishing me a Happy New Year, sir. I hope it comes true and I move to a wider and better pavement!